A Beadwork Companion

A Step by Step Illustrated Workbook for Beading Projects

**Written and Illustrated
by Jean Heinbuch**

Eagle's View Publishing Company
6756 North Fork Road
Liberty, UT 84310

ISBN: 0-943604-31-1
Library of Congress Catalog Card Number: 90-86225

Acknowledgements

I wish to express my thanks to my editor, Denise Knight, for her work on the manuscript and to Brenda Jensen and Kris Sweat for proofing the manuscript and offering suggestions.

FIRST EDITION

10 9 8 7 6 5 4 3 2

TABLE OF CONTENTS

Strike a Light Bag
Pages 36 - 42

Neck Knife Sheath
Pages 54 - 62

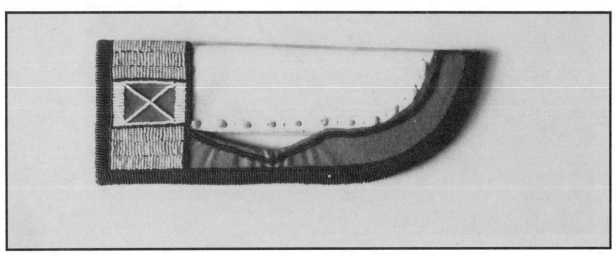

Wrap Around Knife Sheath
Pages 73 - 83

INTRODUCTION

Since first introduced by Columbus in 1492, glass trade beads and beaded articles have held a fascination for all Americans . . . Native and non-Native alike. Until the mid-1960s, the vast majority of beadwork was made by a few Native Americans who had generations of traditions to rely upon for inspiration and instruction. While it is still true that most beadwork on sale is Indian-made, a growing number of Americans and Europeans have become interested in this art form and in learning to make their own beadwork. The materials are easy to locate, but many beginners (and even those with a few pieces under their belts) find that deciding upon exactly the right project is a major obstacle.

Native American design concepts differ greatly from those of European descent and can be difficult to master. The beginning beadworker will often expend tremendous effort completing a piece only to find that, though the piece is technically well made, it doesn't seem quite right. Or, craftworkers try to copy old pieces made by master beaders and find that these pieces represent such a high level of achievement that beginners cannot hope to accomplish good copies. Both paths lead to a great deal of frustration.

In this book, it is hoped that readers will find the information needed to become adept at doing beadwork and that the projects presented will give them enough practice with the materials and concepts to provide a basis for successfully creating original pieces. To this end, the book contains explicit directions and patterns for beading projects of graduating complexity. They are, with a few rather modern exceptions, traditional patterns which have been adapted to modern tastes and uses.

It would be a good idea for everyone using this book (even the experienced beadworker) to read all the instructions thoroughly. The basic instructions at the front of the book will familiarize the reader with the terminology and methods to be used. The projects themselves have been selected to familiarize the reader with certain aspects and problems associated with the craft of beadwork, as well as the principles for laying out designs, which are the foundation of good beadwork. For this reason, the instructions for each project will attempt to explain the best course to follow and why. Design layout and craft pitfalls will be demonstrated wherever possible. The use of this approach should give the beadworker a good comprehension of the art and a "feel" for the designs involved.

BASIC MATERIALS AND TECHNIQUES

A list of supplies which change from project to project is given at the start of each chapter. The Materials section is a list and discussion of the tools and materials common to most of the projects, and in the interest of brevity they will not be discussed again. These items should always be on hand when working on a project.

Frequently used sewing and beading techniques are described in the following sections. When these techniques are used in a project they are identified by the use of capital letters (e.g. Two Bead Return Stitch). This indicates the reader should refer back to these sections for details on the specific technique referenced.

MATERIALS

Beads - Glass seed beads are manufactured in a number of countries. The most uniform come from Czechoslovakia. These beads are usually strung on cotton thread and are sold in bunches called "hanks." Packages of loose seed beads are also sold in many general craft stores; these are usually from the Far East and are less uniform in size and shape. They can easily be used, but the craftsperson using non-Czech beads must carefully select the beads to be used and there will be more waste than when using Czech beads.

All bead producing countries size their beads differently. The projects in this book generally specify size 12/° Czech beads, but if Oriental beads are used, size 13/° or slightly smaller should be used. A size 4/° Italian bead, though a bit on the small side, can also be used. The amount of beads needed for each project is given in hanks. An entire hank of any one color is seldom needed for a project in this book, however it can be difficult to match beads made in different lots and it is best to purchase more than enough beads at the start. A hank is approximately equal to one ounce of loose beads.

When purchasing beads by the ounce, be sure to get at least a half ounce; if greater amounts are needed for a project, this will be indicated.

Thread - There are three choices here: The first and most commonly used is Nymo beading thread, size OO or A. This is a multifilament nylon thread and is fairly easy to use, requiring only infrequent waxing. Silk thread can also be used in size A, or size B if size A is not available. Although silk thread is a good choice for those who wish to do beadwork using traditional materials, it is very prone to fray and must be kept waxed constantly. A third choice is cotton thread; this is another standby for those who do restorations and reproductions. Some beadworkers prefer it because it does not have the "give" of a nylon thread. Note that pure cotton thread should be used and not the polyester wrapped kind which is very inferior for hand sewing.

Wax: Beading thread must be waxed to prevent tangles. Pure beeswax is most often used, but some beadworkers prefer to use the waxes made for skiers. This is largely a matter of personal choice so try both to see which is preferable.

Sharps Beading Needles: This book deals with beads that will take a size #12 Sharps needle easily.

Glover's Needles: Sizes #6, #7 or #8 will handle any of the tougher leather construction jobs such as knife sheaths and belts which require the use of heavier threads.

Ruler and Compass: Nice straight lines and "true" circles are essential for good beadwork.

Marking Pen: Be sure to get the felt tip kind with indelible ink and either a "razor" or "ultra fine" point.

Scissors: To work on leather, a pair of leather shears is indispensable. Lighter shears will warp if used consistently on leather. A good pair of scissors for cutting thread and fabric is also necessary. Use whatever size feels comfortable as they will be in use a great deal.

Round Awl: This is for punching the holes necessary for constructing the projects. The round type, which separates the leather fibers, is preferable to the square or three cornered types, which cut the fibers and thereby weaken the leather.

Leather Punch: Holes needed for general construction of pieces can also be made with a leather punch. In some cases this will save time and effort.

Leather or Fabric for Beading: Although the proper beading material will be listed for each project, this seems the best place to elaborate on their different qualities. For the most part, beading materials are interchangeable, but keep in mind that beadwork done on fabrics will usually have to be mounted on a leather base for strength.

When beading directly on leather, brain-tanned hides are strongly suggested. They cost considerably more than commercially tanned hides, but the final product is correctly made and looks it! In addition to aesthetic considerations, brain-tanned leather is much easier to work on and will result in faster work and fewer errors. The quality of the hide fibers allows for much smaller stitching - the hallmark of good beadwork. If, because of economics or availability, brain-tanned hides are not possible, commercially tanned buckskin may, of course, be used. An even better alternative is for the craftworker to learn to make their own brain-tanned leather. Instructions for brain tanning may be found in *A Quillwork Companion*, also by Jean Heinbuch.

Leather has two sides; the flesh side which was next to the muscles of the animal and is the rougher of the two sides and the grain side which had the hair on it before tanning and is the smoother side. Beads are usually sewn to the grain side of the leather.

Wool and velvet are the fabrics chosen by most beadworkers and working with both of them is interesting. When wool is used, especially red wool, the color of the fabric is usually worked into the design, saving some effort on the craftworker's part. Fabric is quite easy to work on freehand, but some people prefer to mount it in an embroiderer's hoop; if trouble is experienced in maintaining lines or keeping the piece flat, give the hoop a try. Muslin is often used to cover the back of beadwork pieces.

Pattern Making: The pattern(s) for the projects are provided on grids where one square is equal to one square inch. Where possible, they are given full size. Transfer the pattern to heavy paper or Mylar (thin plastic) to make a pattern that will stand up to years of hard use. If the pattern is shown full size it can be traced directly onto paper or by using carbon paper between the book and the pattern paper or Mylar. If the pattern is not given on a one to one basis, simply make a one inch grid and amplify the pattern by hand. Cross the grid squares at the same places in both patterns.

CONSTRUCTION STITCHES

The sewing techniques needed to make the projects in this book are described below. Practice them on some scraps before starting a project if they are not familiar. Remember, the closer and finer the stitching, the better the end result.

The same sturdy **Backstitch Knot** is used throughout the book to secure the ends of the thread, in both the beading and the construction of the projects. A backstitch is made by pointing the needle back towards the the beginning of the stitch so that the thread beneath the surface passes under the thread on the surface. A Backstitch Knot at the end of a stretch of sewing or beading consists of three tiny backstitches in the leather or fabric (Figure I-1). The stitches

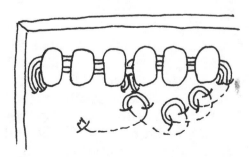

Figure I-1

should be hidden under the beadwork or taken along the very edge of a row. Trim the end of the thread flush with the surface of the work. Notice how the thread crosses within the fabric in the completed knot. To start a new piece of thread place an overhand knot in the end of the thread (Figure I-2) and take an initial stitch to hold the thread in place until the three stabilizing stitches can be taken.

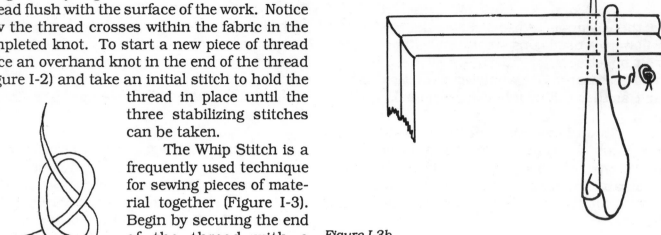

Figure I-3b

The Whip Stitch is a frequently used technique for sewing pieces of material together (Figure I-3). Begin by securing the end of the thread with a Backstitch Knot; the best place for this knot is usually on the back of the work. Next pass the needle and thread through the two (or more) pieces from front to back (Figure I-3a). Pull the thread tight, bring the needle and thread over the top of the

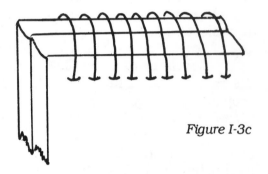

Figure I-2

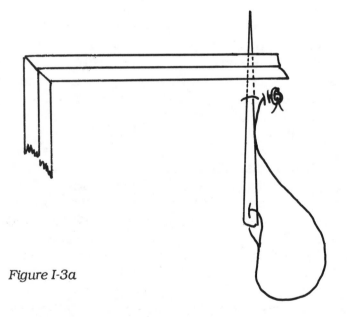

Figure I-3a

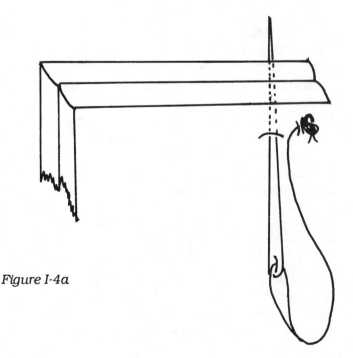

Figure I-3c

(Figure I-4a). Pull the thread tight and then run the needle through the material from back to front, which is the reverse of the first stitch (Figure I-4b). Continue stitching back and forth

Figure I-4a

pieces of material, and take another stitch from front to back (Figure 1-3b). Continue in this way until the sewing is finished (Figure 1-3c) and tie the thread off with a Back Stitch Knot.

The Running Stitch is shown in Figure 1-4. Once again, begin by securing the end of the thread with a Backstitch Knot. Pass the needle through the leather or fabric from front to back

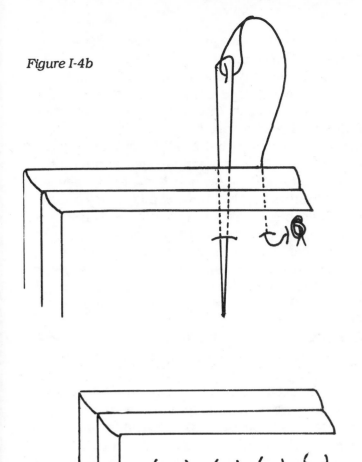

Figure I-4b

Figure I-4c

through the material until the sewing is completed (Figure I-4c) and then secure the end of the thread with another Backstitch Knot.

Close spacing of the stitching in both these techniques is very important in making the seams look neat. The Running Stitch should seldom be spaced with more than 1/8 inch between the individual stitches and 1/16 inch spacing is preferable for the Whip Stitch.

BEADING TECHNIQUES

Use a double thread for sewn beadwork and tie the ends together with a simple overhand knot (see Figure I-2). Secure both ends of the thread with a Backstitch Knot in the leather or fabric as described in the preceding section on construction techniques. By using a fine thread (size A or OO) and doubling it, the thread will still fit through the beads and the beads will be not fall off if one of the thread strands breaks. Beads are sewn to the smoother or grain side of leather and

to the right side of fabrics. It is not necessary to knot the thread at the end of each row of beads; this wastes time that is better spent beading.

It is also not necessary to stitch all the way through the fabric or leather when beading, though some craftworkers do. Try both ways when practicing. Keep in mind that passing the thread completely through the leather will be unhandy at times and any article that is sewn together before the beadwork begins will have to be worked from the surface. In situations such as this, the long fibers of brain tanned leather are a definite advantage, as they hold small surface stitches best and make the work much easier. Longer stitches may be needed on commercially tanned leather.

The Three Bead Return Stitch is the most commonly used beading stitch in this book. A variation of this stitch, using just two beads, is also used frequently. This Two Bead Return Stitch is employed in small areas of beadwork or on tight curves where three beads will not maintain a nice straight line. Reducing the number of beads per stitch remedies this problem.

Start the Three Bead Return Stitch (Figure I-5) by stringing three beads on the needle and

Figure I-5

thread. Take a small backstitch in the leather, emerging between the first and second beads. Thread the needle through the second and third beads a second time. Add three more beads to the thread and repeat the backstitch, returning the thread through the second and third beads. Continue in this manner as long as necessary. For the Two Bead Return Stitch, string two beads on the thread and make the return stitch through just the last bead.

One special note when working either Return Stitch in a circle: before beginning a new row, pass the thread through the first bead in the row just completed (A in Figure I-6). Then take a small stitch from the outside of this previous row (point B) to the inside (point C) and begin the new row at this point. This method will maintain

Figure I-6

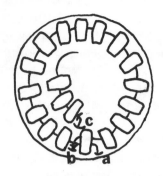

circular rows. If the rows are worked in a spiral fashion, it is very difficult to keep the circle from becoming an oval and the result is many times less tidy.

The Gourd Stitch (also referred to as the Peyote Stitch) may be used as either a main beading technique or as a seam cover. As a main beading technique, it is most often used to bead around cylindrical objects such as barette sticks, key chains, fan handles and pipe stems to name just a few. Usually the object is covered with fabric or leather and the first row of beads is stitched down with a Two Bead Return Stitch (top of Figure I-7). There must be an even number of beads in this row. The spacing between the beads in the illustration has been kept wide so that the technique will be clear,

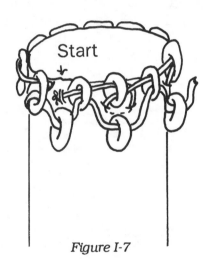

Start

Figure I-7

but in reality, the beads should fit snugly against each other.

After the last return stitch in the first row add a single bead to the thread. Without taking a stitch in the material, pass the thread through the first bead in the first row and pull the thread snug. Pick up another single bead. Pass the thread through the third bead in the first row, skipping the second bead, which is anchored by a return stitch. Pull the thread snug. Add another single bead and pass the thread through the fifth bead in the first row. Continue adding single beads to the second row, skipping every

other bead in the first row. There are half as many beads in the second row as in the first and there will be spaces between the new beads. Start the third row by adding a single bead and passing the thread through the first bead in the second row. Pull the thread snug, setting the new bead in position between the first and last beads in the second row. Pick up a single bead and pass the thread through the second bead in the second row. Continue in this manner all the way around the object being beaded. The third and all subsequent rows have the same number of beads as in the second row. In these rows the thread passes through *each* bead in the previous row. The new beads in each row fit into the spaces left between beads in the previous row, creating the network effect. End with a Backstitch Knot as previously described. The Gourd Stitch should be practiced by beginning beadworkers before it is used in an actual project.

The Lazy Stitch (Figure I-8) is the final method of beading dealt with in this book. Begin this stitch by picking up the number of beads required to run all the way across the row to be beaded. Then take a small stitch along the opposite edge of the row, to the point where the next string of beads is to be placed. Pull the thread snug. Add the next string of beads and take a stitch beside the starting point. This completes two beading stitches; repeat this procedure until the row to be beaded is finished. The

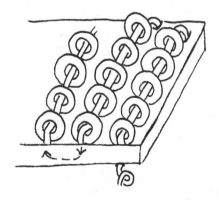

Figure I-8

Lazy Stitch can be worked either horizontally or vertically.

To maintain a neat tidy appearance, pay close attention to three things while working the Lazy Stitch. First, use rows that are 1/2 inch wide or less (5 to 10 beads). Second, make sure that the stitches are parallel to one another and pulled to a uniform tightness, with the beads snug against one another. Finally, more than one Lazy Stitch row is usually used to cover a section. Align the stitches in each row with the stitches from the previous row so that there is a straight line of beads all the way across or down the section.

BEADED EDGES

As in all craftwork, the finishing touches on a piece of beadwork are very important. No matter how much time and effort are put into the main design, the piece will not look complete until the edges are finished. Sometimes this is done with a fabric binding, but very often the edges of a piece of beadwork are also beaded. Four forms of beaded edging are described for use on the projects in this book: Oblique Edging, Loop Edging, a Lazy Stitch Seam Cover and a Gourd Stitch Seam Cover.

Oblique Edging (Figure I-9) is a variation of the Two Bead Return Stitch. Begin by picking up two beads on the needle and thread. Then take a stitch back to the start and pass the thread through the first bead again. Pick up a third bead and then pass the thread through the second

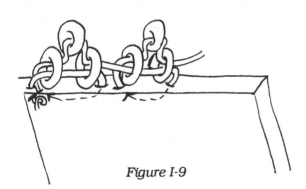

Figure I-9

bead, completing the first stitch. Add two more beads to the thread and repeat the stitch.

Loop Edging (Figure I-10) is a great favorite with beadworkers. Though it seems fairly straight forward, it takes some practice to get the spacing right. This technique can be done with any number of beads; the correct number is given for each of the projects in which it is used. For a practice piece, put six beads on the thread. Look at Figure 10 and notice that the trick is to take the stitch in such a way that the two top beads are

squeezed to the top of the stitch. For the first stitch squeeze the two middle beads to the top. After taking the stitch, pass the thread through the last two beads again and add four new beads. Again take a stitch, this time squeezing the first two beads to the top of the stitch. Pass the thread through the last two beads and repeat this ma-

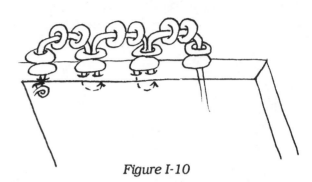

Figure I-10

neuver until the edging is complete.

A variation of the Lazy Stitch can also be used to cover seams (Figure I-11). Start by picking up enough beads to completely cover the seam so that none of the stitching shows. Run the beads over the seam to the opposite side of the work and take a stitch. Pick up the same number of beads for the second row and run them over the seam to the beginning side and take another stitch. Repeat this procedure, going back and forth over the seam, until the end of the seam is reached.

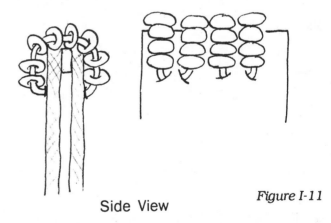

Side View

Figure I-11

The Gourd Stitch may also be worked on a flat surface and used to cover a seam (Figure I-12). As before, stitch the first row down with a Two Bead Return Stitch. In this variation however, take a small stitch in the material at the end of the first row. Pick up a single bead and pass the thread through the second to last bead in the first row. As before, skip the bead that was caught by the return stitch. Continue in this manner, adding single beads and passing the thread through every other bead in the first row until the end of the second row is reached. Take a small stitch at the end of the second row. Pick up single beads and pass the thread through each bead of the second row. In this manner the network begins to form. Continue working the rows back and forth until the edge is covered. When the final row of beads is completed, stitch each bead in this last row to the back side of the piece. This holds the edging firmly in place.

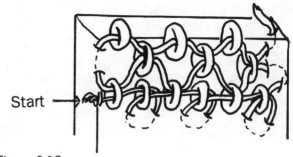

Start

Figure I-12

LARGE BARRETTE

Materials

2	Buckskin Pieces - 5" x 5"
1	Small Buckskin Piece - 1" x 1 1/4"
1	Medium Weight Cowhide Piece - 5" x 5"
1	6" Wood Dowel - 1/4" round; pointed at one end
1	Bobbin Nymo Beading Thread - Size A
1	Tube Contact Cement
3	Hanks Size 12/° Seed Beads:
	1 Dark Red, 1 Apple Green & 1 White

This first project gives an introduction to straight forward geometric designs. Based on simple numerical progressions, geometric designs are very common in Native American art. This design, while used by many tribes, has a very midwestern flavor. The simplicity of the design allows the beginner to develop skills in manipulating the materials involved in the craft of beading.

CONSTRUCTION

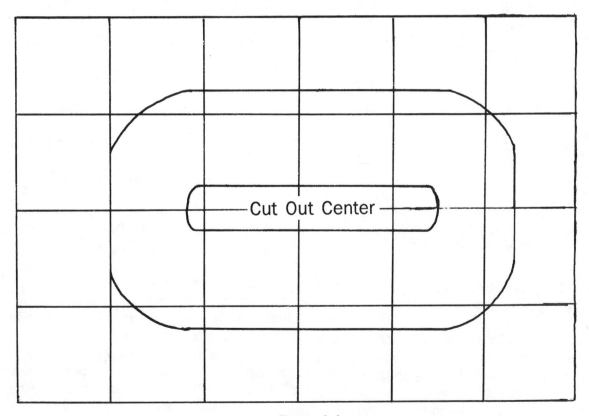

Cut Out Center

Figure 1-1

The pattern for this barrette is provided on a grid in Figure 1-1 where one square is equal to one square inch. Trace the pattern onto the piece of cowhide and cut it out. This cowhide piece is called a blank and it stiffens the barrette when sewn between the pieces of buckskin.

The buckskin pieces must be cut slightly larger than the blank, so place the pattern on each of them and draw a line on the leather which is 1/8 inch out from the edge of the pattern. Cut the two buckskin pieces out along these lines.

Sandwich the cowhide blank between the two buckskin pieces and stitch the edges of the buckskin together with a Whip Stitch. Stitch the outside edges first, then sew the inside edges

Figure 1-2

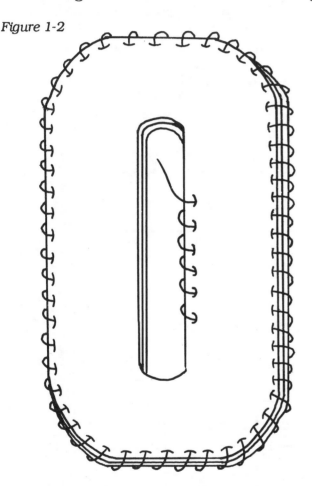

around the center cutout (Figure 1-2). Keep the stitches as small as possible and space them close together.

Glue the small piece of buckskin onto the last inch of the blunt end of the wooden rod. If necessary, trim the edges running up the stick to make them fit smoothly around the rod. Whip Stitch the edges together as shown in Figure 1-3.

Figure 1-3

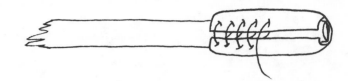

BEADING INSTRUCTIONS

The design pattern for this barrette is illustrated in Figure 1-4. It will be helpful to refer to it as the beading progresses.

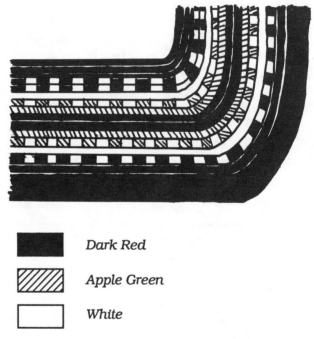

■ Dark Red

▨ Apple Green

☐ White

Figure 1-4

Begin beading on the inner edge (Figure 1-5), using a Three Bead Return Stitch on the straight parts and a Two Bead Return Stitch on the tight curves. Since the barrette is already constructed, it will be necessary to bead on the surface of the buckskin.

Bead three rows (ovals) of dark red beads from the inner edge out. In the next two rows, alternate two beads of dark red with two beads of white. Add one row of white beads.

In the next row (the 7th), alternate two beads of apple green with two white beads and match the white and green areas in this row with the corresponding white and red areas in the 4th and 5th rows. It will be impossible to maintain

Figure 1-5

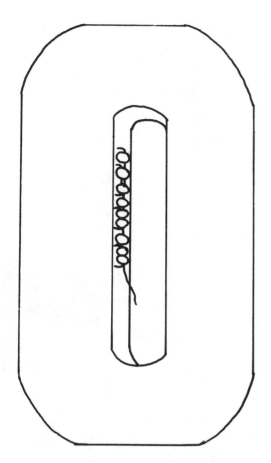

alternating two beads of dark red with 2 or 3 white beads as needed to match the white and colored areas in the other rows. It will now be necessary to add extra white beads in the straight work as well as on the curves. It may even be necessary to use more than 3 white beads in a few places, but the number of red beads should remain constant at two.

Finish the main beadwork with one row of dark red beads.

Bead the outside edge of the barrette with a Lazy Stitch Seam Cover (Figure 1-6) and dark red beads. Start anywhere on the outside edge, next to the beadwork just completed, and string on enough beads to cover all the stitching on both sides of the piece. Seven beads should be about the proper number. Run the beads over the edge of the seam and take a small stitch on the back of

the alternating color pattern on the curves without periodically adding a third bead. This is best done with white beads, as a white bead will be much less noticeable than a colored one.

The number of times an extra bead needs to be added will increase as the work moves further from the center. This is done to keep the pattern from becoming confusing or random in appearance. Look at the photograph of this project (*Page 13*) and note the bead additions as the rows move further from the center of the piece. This is a good technique to remember when working any beading project, as the problem is a common one.

Continue beading with one row of apple green beads followed by two rows of dark red beads and another row of apple green beads.

Alternate two beads each of apple green and white in the next row (the 12th). Again match the white and colored areas in this row with those in rows 4, 5 and 7 as closely as possible. Add white beads on the curves where needed to maintain the overall design.

Add one row of white beads and then a row

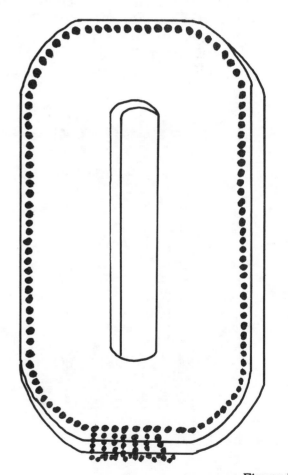

Figure 1-6

the barrette. Add the next string of beads to the thread, lay them around the edge of the barrette and take the next stitch on the front next to the main beadwork. Continue in this manner all the way around the barrette. Secure the end of the thread with a Backstitch Knot.

Bead the leather on the wooden rod with a Gourd Stitch. This stitch is described in the Beading Techniques section at the beginning of the book. Follow the bead graph in Figure 1-7; in this graph each square represents a single bead. Begin on the bottom edge of the leather and bead up towards the top of the rod (Figures 1-8 and 1-9). Stitch a first row of dark red beads to the leather with a Two Bead Return Stitch, making sure there are an even number of beads in the row. Add a second row of dark red. Start by picking up a single bead and passing the thread through the first bead in the first row. Add another bead to the thread and pass the needle through the third bead in the first row. Continue adding single beads and passing the thread through the beads in the first row which are not anchored by a return stitch. There are half as many beads in the second row as in the first. Note that in the graph the first row is staggered and appears to be two rows. This is because the beads not anchored by a return stitch are pulled up-

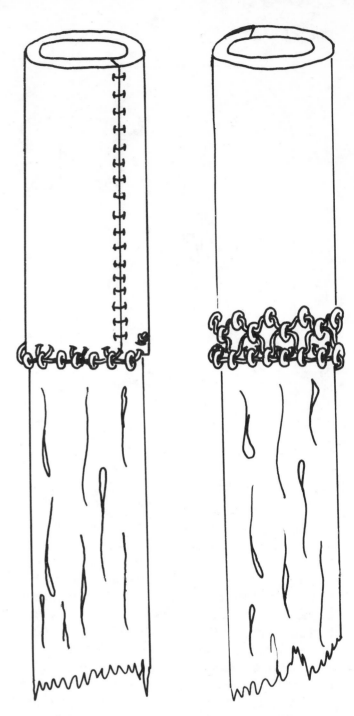

Figure 1-8   Figure 1-9

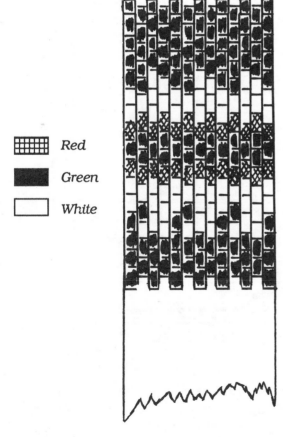

Figure 1-7

Red

Green

White

ward when the second row is added, making the first two rows appear to be three rows.

The third row is also dark red. In this row, add a new bead between each bead in the second row. That is, pick up a single bead and pass the thread through the first bead in the second row. Then pick up a single bead and pass the thread through the second bead in the second row and so on. There are the same number of beads in the second row as in the third. All subsequent rows are added in exactly the same manner as the third row. Add two more rows of dark red beads (rows 4 & 5), then a single row of white beads (row 6).

In the next two rows, alternate one dark red bead and one white bead (rows 7 & 8). Add three rows of white beads (rows 9, 10 & 11); two rows of apple green beads (rows 12 & 13); three rows of dark red beads (rows 14, 15 & 16); and two more rows of apple green beads (rows 17 & 18).

Continue with three rows of white beads (rows 19 & 20) and then two rows of alternating one dark red bead with one white bead (rows 21 & 22).

Finish with approximately eight rows of dark red beads. The last row should be just above the top edge of the leather. Pass the thread through this row a second time for extra strength. Pull the thread slightly so that the top beads draw closer together and fold over the top edge a little, giving the end a nice finished look (Figure 1-10). Secure the end of the thread by taking three or four small backstitches in the leather (a Backstitch Knot) under the beadwork and trim off any remaining thread.

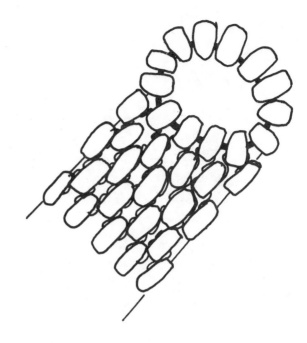

Figure 1-10

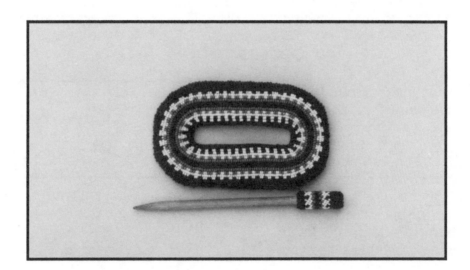

HEART-SHAPED BARRETTE

Materials

2	Buckskin Pieces - 4" x 5"
1	Small Buckskin Piece - 1" x 1 1/4"
1	Medium Weight Cowhide Piece - 4" x 5"
1	6" Wood Dowel - 1/4" round; pointed at one end
1	Bobbin Nymo Beading Thread - Size A
1	Tube Contact Cement
2	Hanks Size 12/° Cut Seed Beads:
	1 Bright Red & 1 Medium Blue
2	Hanks Size 12/° Seed Beads:
	1 Bright Yellow & 1 White

The pattern and design of this piece display an entirely modern influence, such as will be found at many trading posts. Pieces such as this are very popular and are commonly seen in everyday use. The beadwork will present novice craftworkers with an opportunity to stretch their technical ability a bit. Several principles; namely crowding, stretching and bead row organization are involved.

CONSTRUCTION

The pattern for this barrette is provided on a grid in Figure 2-1 where one square is equal to one square inch. Trace the pattern onto the cowhide piece and then onto the two pieces of buckskin. Cut the buckskin pieces about 1/8 inch larger than the cowhide piece in all directions. The cowhide fits between the buckskin pieces as a stiffener for the barrette and the buckskin pieces are easier to sew together if they are slightly larger.

Start on the top outside edge, in the middle of the barrette, and use a Whip Stitch to sew the two pieces of buckskin together around the cowhide piece (Figure 2-2). It is not necessary to catch the cowhide in the stitching. Keep the stitches as small and even as possible and space them close together. After completing the outside edge, sew the edges of the cutout sections using the same stitching technique.

Next, glue the small piece of buckskin onto

Figure 2-1

the last inch of the blunt end of the wooden rod and Whip Stitch the edges running up the stick together (Figure 2-3). Trim the edges if necessary to make them fit smoothly.

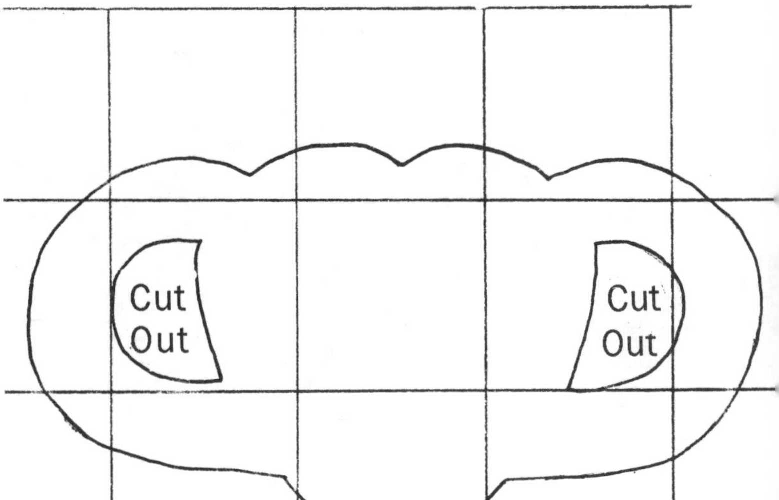

Figure 2-2

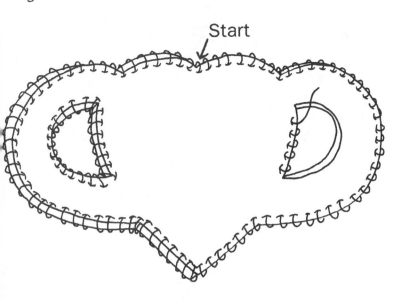

Start

Figure 2-3

INITIAL BEADING

A diagram showing the locations and colors of the bead rows on the barrette is provided in Figure 2-4. It will be helpful to refer to this as the beading progresses. All beading must be done on the surface of the leather. Because of the small size of the piece and the intricacies of the beading, use a Two Bead Return Stitch on the entire barrette.

Begin beading on the outside edge, at the top of the leather heart shape (point A in Figure 2-5). Bead one row of blue cut seed beads around the outside edge of the heart until the top is reached once again (point B).

Before starting the second row, take a small stitch in the leather. Start this stitch by the last bead in the first row (point C in Figure 2-6) and end it where the first bead in the second row should be placed (point D). This technique is similar to the method described for circular objects in the Techniques section and has the same purpose. The stitch in the leather keeps the outside rows of the heart shape aligned properly, which helps keep the integrity of the design intact.

Continue outlining the large heart with two rows of white seed beads, followed by another row of blue cut seed beads. Take a stitch in the leather at the end of each row.

LAYOUT

Center the interior design within the space remaining on the inside of the heart. This design is reproduced on a small grid of five squares per inch (Figure 2-7). It can be traced onto a piece of paper, then cut out and drawn around, or it can be copied freehand onto the leather. This last method is preferable, as it allows greater flexibility in correcting any minor flaws in the symmetry

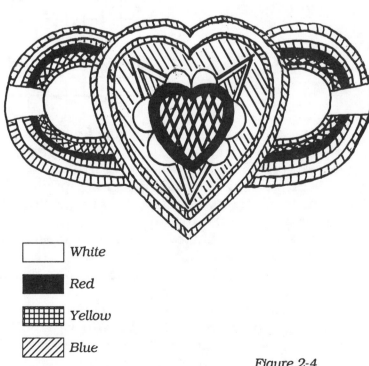

☐ *White*

■ *Red*

▦ *Yellow*

▨ *Blue*

Figure 2-4

Figure 2-5

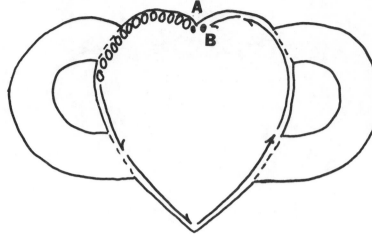

Figure 2-6

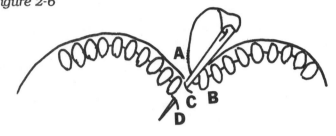

Figure 2-7

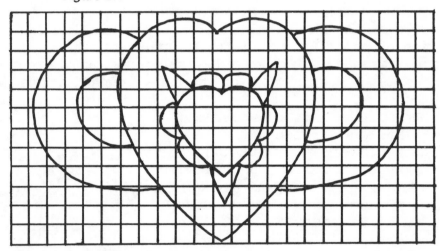

of the piece. Draw the heart shape first, then draw the three points on the sides and bottom of the heart and lastly, the white petal shapes.

In planning the beading for this interior design, great care was taken to organize the manner in which the rows of beads should be applied, so that the limited space would be used to best advantage. For instance, the outside row of the heart shape follows the guideline around the design, and all subsequent rows inside of this are also beaded following the outer shape of the design. This same procedure is followed with the white petal shapes around the outside of the interior heart. This curved application of the beads reinforces the rounded elements of the design.

The three blue points, which are linear in design, are beaded differently. The guidelines are beaded with white beads, but then the blue fill is worked in rows running straight across the points. This maintains the sharp definition of these angular shapes, and the linear application of beads reinforces the linear elements of the design.

Always pay attention to the organization of the rows in planning and making a piece of beadwork, as applying the beads in different directions makes great differences in the appearance of the finished product.

BEADING INSTRUCTIONS

To start the interior design, bead around the guideline drawn for the interior heart shape, outlining it with two rows of red cut seed beads (Figure 2-8). Take a small stitch in the leather between each row as was done when beading the exterior heart. Follow the outline of the first rows

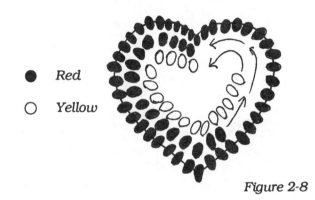

● Red

○ Yellow

Figure 2-8

and fill the remainder of the interior heart with about four rows of yellow seed beads.

As the beadwork nears the center of the design, the heart will start to lose some of its definition and the spacing will become so tight that the placement of the rows must be adjusted to compensate. At this point fill the remaining space as neatly as possible, placing the beads in positions compatible with the rest of the design.

Figure 2-9

● *Blue*   ○ *White*

The handling of small, tight spaces such as this varies greatly from piece to piece, but as experience is gained in working with beads, problems such as this will be easy to overcome.

Next, bead a white outline around one of the petal shapes. Take a small stitch at the end of the row, reverse direction, and fill the rest of the petal with approximately three rows of white beads which follow the direction of the outline (Figure 2-9). Once again, as the center of the area is reached, it may be necessary to vary the position of the final few beads to completely fill the space.

Complete the other five petals in the same manner as the first. It is possible to move from one petal in a pair to the other without knotting off the thread, but secure the end before moving to another pair.

Bead a white outline around one of the points, beginning next to the red heart (point A in Figure 2-9) and ending next to it again at point B. Fill in the triangular design with five to six straight rows of blue beads, beading *across* the triangle. Repeat this procedure on the other two points to complete the beading of the interior design.

Bead the background area, between the interior design and the outline of the large leather heart shape, with a Two Bead Return Stitch and blue cut seed beads. The interior design will break up the fill work, so work the background in sections.

Start at the top, on one side of the beaded outline of the large heart, and apply rows of blue beads, horizontally back and forth, filling from the top of the heart towards the bottom (Figure 2-10). Run the rows between the edges of the large heart and the edges of the interior design. This

Figure 2-10

area is small enough that it should be easy to take a stitch through the leather to start each new row. Bead down one side of the barrette and back up the other.

While filling the background, there will be many areas where it is difficult to properly space the beads. It will be necessary at times to crowd an extra bead into what seems a tight area, or if this is not possible, to space several beads over an area that seems a bit large. These principles are called crowding and stretching and often occur in a piece that is asymmetrical.

When an extra bead needs to be crowded into a space, the Three Bead Return Stitch can often be used effectively. However, if the third bead bunches the stitch up and forms a bit of a lump in the work, pull the stitch out and return to the Two Bead variation. In this case, make the initial stitch so that it covers a slightly larger area and use the return stitch to space the beads evenly over this area.

Bead the edge of the large heart with a Loop Edging Stitch. Start just to the left of the center of the heart on the bottom (Figure 2-11). Secure the thread on the front edge of the piece with a Backstitch Knot. For the first loop, place seven beads on the thread, take a small stitch from the front of the piece to the back, forcing the

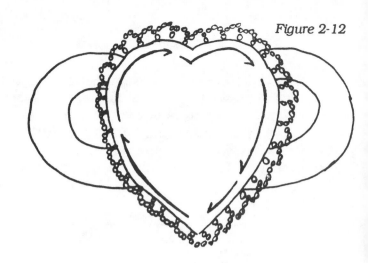

Figure 2-12

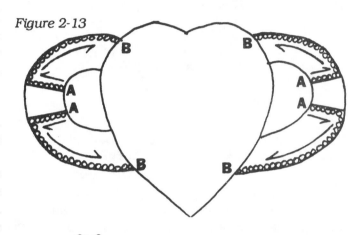

Figure 2-13

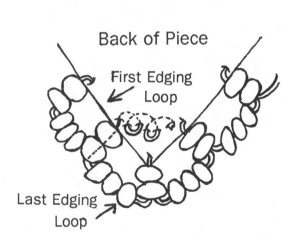

Back of Piece

First Edging Loop

Last Edging Loop

Figure 2-11

Figure 2-14

middle three beads to the top of the stitch. Return the thread through the last two beads. Add five beads to the thread for all subsequent loops, take a small stitch which leaves the first three beads at the top and pass the thread through the last two beads.

Bead all the way around the outside edge of the leather heart (Figure 2-12). In the areas where the outer loops of the barrette join the heart, make the small stitches in the surface of the leather, rather than passing the thread from front to back.

To finish the edging, add three beads for the last loop, then pass the thread through the first two beads of the first loop. Take a small stitch on the back of the piece and knot the thread with a Backstitch Knot (see Figure 2-11).

Before beading the rest of the barrette (the outer loops), insert the wooden dowel through the cut out sections of the leather, passing it under

18

the heart. Mark the areas of the loops which the stick passes over with a marking pen. These areas will be left unbeaded except for the outside edging. The diagram in Figure 2-4 shows the placement of these marks.

The lines just drawn divide each loop into two sections. Start on the inside edge of one of these lines (point A in Figure 2-13). Bead from the inside out with blue beads and a Two Bead Return Stitch, being careful to cover the line. Continue to bead around the outside edge of this loop section with a single row of blue beads, ending at the intersection with the leather heart (point B).

Bead a second row of blue around the outside edge only. Continue beading back and forth, parallel to the edge, and fill in this section of the loop with the following color sequence: two rows white; one row blue; one row red; one row yellow; and approximately three rows of blue beads. The last row of blue should be on the inside (cut out) edge of the loop.

Bead the other three sections of the loops in the exactly the same manner.

Edge the outside of both barrette loops, including the edges of the blank areas, with the same Loop Edging Stitch used for the heart (Figure 2-14). The entire outer edge can be beaded because the stick will not touch this edge when it is in the barrette. Again, start with a Backstitch Knot and use blue beads, with seven in the first loop and five in subsequent loops. Place the first and last loops on each side behind the edging of the large heart. Knot the thread on the back of the piece with a Backstitch Knot.

The final step is beading the leather on the wooden rod to create the barrette stick. Use a Gourd Stitch (described in the Beading Techniques section) and stitch the first row to the bottom of the leather with a Two Bead Return Stitch (Figures 2-15 and 2-16). Use blue beads and make sure there are an even number of beads in this row. Add a second row of blue beads in the network style of this stitch, using half as many beads as in the first row. Continue in this manner, adding three more rows of blue beads.

In the next two rows (6 and 7), alternate one white bead and one blue bead around the stick. Follow this with two rows alternating first one blue bead and then one white bead.

Bead the next two rows (10 & 11) alternating one red bead with one blue bead, then add two rows alternating one yellow bead and one red

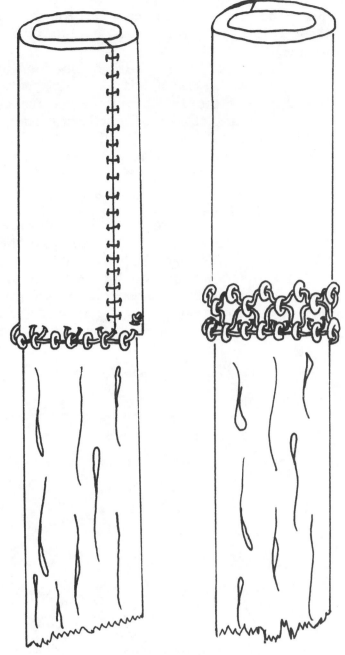

Figure 2-15   Figure 2-16

bead. Follow this with two rows alternating one red bead and one yellow bead. Then add another two rows alternating one yellow bead and one red bead.

In the next two rows (18 &19), alternate one blue bead and one red bead. Follow this with two rows alternating one blue bead and one white bead, then switch order and add two rows alternating one white bead with one blue bead.

Add three rows of blue beads (rows 24, 25 & 26), then two rows of red beads and two rows of yellow beads. Finish with approximately five rows of blue beads; the last row should reach just

19

above the top of the leather. Run the thread through this last row a second time for added strength.

Finish the barrette stick by making the tassel loops on the end of the stick. To make the first loop, take the thread from the last row of gourd stitch and string on the following beads: six blue, four red, four yellow, three blue, four white, three blue, four white, three blue, four yellow, four red and six blue. Pass the thread through the next bead in the final row of gourd stitch beadwork (Figure 2-17).

To make the second loop, add the same sequence of beads to the thread, then pass the thread through the next bead in line on the stick. Continue in this way around the stick, until the last loop of the tassel passes through the last bead in the gourd stitch row. Knot the thread with a Backstitch Knot on the leather, hiding it in the gourd stitch beadwork.

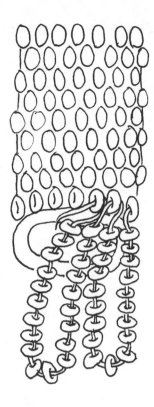

Figure 2-17

ROSETTE HAIR TIES

Materials
4   Buckskin Circles - 3" diameter
2   Medium to Heavy Weight Cowhide Circles - 2 1/4" diameter
2   Buckskin Thongs - 12" long
1   Bobbin Nymo Beading Thread - Size A

5   Hanks Size 12/° Seed Beads:
        1 Transparent Dark Blue, 1 Light Blue,
        1 Lavender, 1 Transparent Pink, & 1 White

The design for this project is fairly intricate and the pattern requires carefully drawn guidelines in several places. Pay close attention to the layout instructions, as the same principles apply to the layout of all geometric designs. Once some experience is gained with these layout methods, it should be easy for the reader to apply the same principles to new ideas of their own. In this project, the design is beaded before the pieces of the rosette are sewn together.

INITIAL LAYOUT

Layout the design for this project on two of the 3 inch circles of buckskin. These will be the front or beaded sides of the rosettes. It is a good idea to put several layers of masking tape on the back or flesh sides of these pieces before beginning to work. This stabilizes the leather and gives a firmer work surface. Remove the tape when the beading is finished.

All the layout steps are done on both pieces of buckskin. To avoid repetition, work on the second piece will not be mentioned again. Begin the layout by drawing the outer sunburst portion of the design on the grain side of the buckskin. Start by making a small dot in the exact center of the circle with a marking pen (point A in Figure 3-1). Then use a compass with a pencil as a marker and draw a 2 1/4 inch diameter circle around the center mark. Go over the pencil lines with the marking pen to make clear guidelines.

Place the point of the compass on the center mark and draw a 1 1/2 inch diameter circle inside the previous one. Trace over this line with the pen.

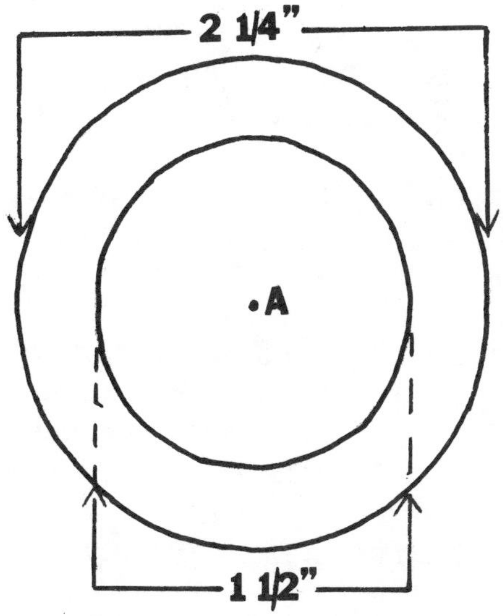

Choose a starting point anywhere on the

Figure 3-1

outer circle and make a small dot. Make marks every 1/2 inch from this point, around half of the outer circle.

Mark the other half of the circle with an equal number of marks, each one straight across from one of the marks already made. To do this, take a ruler and lay it across the circle from the first mark on the outer edge (point B in Figure 3-2), through the center dot (point A). Make a new mark where the ruler crosses the outer circle on the opposite side (point C). Move the ruler to the next mark (point D) and align it through point A again. Make another mark where the ruler crosses the outer circle (point E). Continue around the

Figure 3-3

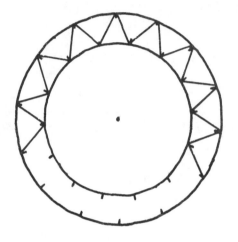

Figure 3-2

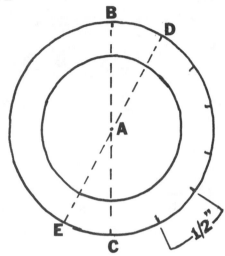

outer circle in this manner until evenly spaced marks are drawn all the way around the circle.

This method of marking the second half of the circle compensates for any small errors made in measuring the first half, evening them out across the circle and minimizing the effects of measuring errors made consistently in the same direction.

Next, find a halfway point between any two of the 1/2 inch marks on the outer circle, place the ruler between this point and the center of the circle, and put a mark on the inner circle where the ruler crosses it. Go halfway around the inner circle making small marks approximately every 3/8 inch. Take great care to center these marks between the 1/2 inch marks on the outer circle. This is more important than having the marks exactly 3/8 inch apart, so make any compensations that seem necessary.

Mark the remaining half of the inner circle in the same manner as the outer circle. Align the ruler from point F (Figure 3-3) through point A and make a mark (point G) where the ruler crosses the opposite side of the inner circle. Move the ruler to the next mark (point H), run it through point A and make a mark on the opposite side at point I. Continue in this manner until the

Figure 3-4

entire inner circle is marked.

Next, draw the guidelines for the sunburst pattern around the outside edge of the rosette by taking the ruler and connecting the marks on the inner and outer circles. Look at Figure 3-4 to be sure that this pattern is drawn correctly.

INITIAL BEADING

A color-keyed diagram of this rosette is provided in Figure 3-5. It will be helpful to refer to it throughout the beading process. To maintain the circular shape of the beadwork, when each row is completed, pass the thread back through the first bead in the row and take a small stitch from the outside of the row to the inside (see Beading Techniques section). Bead the first rosette completely, then repeat the process on the second piece of buckskin.

Start at the outside tip of one of the sunburst points and use a Three Bead Return Stitch to bead around the outside edge of the outer (2 1/4") circle guideline with one row of dark blue beads (Figure 3-6).

Figure 3-5

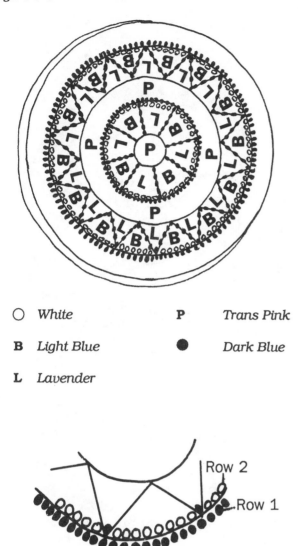

○ White   **P** Trans Pink

B Light Blue   ● Dark Blue

L Lavender

the inside.

The sections of the sunburst which are pointed on the outside and get wider towards the center of the rosette are filled with lavender beads. The sections which are wide on the outside and narrow to a point on the 1 1/2 inch circular guideline are filled with light blue beads. The guidelines separating the sections are outlined with dark blue beads (see Figure 3-5). Keep this in mind while working in towards the center of the rosette.

Start the third and all subsequent rows in the sunburst pattern with a single dark blue bead placed on one of the guidelines. Continue to use a Three Bead Return Stitch. Bead the third row with single lavender beads inside the narrow points, flanked by dark blue beads on the guidelines. Fill the wide sections with light blue beads (Figure 3-7).

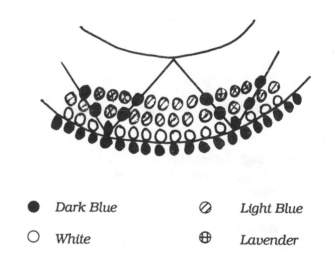

● Dark Blue   ⊘ Light Blue

○ White   ⊕ Lavender

Figure 3-7

Figure 3-6

Start the second row inside the first, at the tip of one of the sunburst points. Continue to use a Three Bead Return Stitch and start with one dark blue bead and two white beads. Place the dark blue bead on the tip of the sunburst point (see Figure 3-6). Follow with stitches of white beads until the next sunburst point is reached. Add a dark blue bead on the tip of the second point. Continue around the circle with white beads between the guidelines and dark blue beads on the tips of the sunburst points. Crowd or stretch the beads where necessary to follow the guidelines exactly. At the end of the row, remember to run the thread through the first bead and take a small stitch from the outside of the row to

Finish the sunburst area between the two circles with lavender, dark blue and light blue beads. Follow the guidelines and the color key in Figure 3-5. This should take about three more rows.

Once the sunburst area is completed, bead three rows of transparent pink beads inside the inner circle. Again, work the rows towards the center of the rosette and take a small stitch at the end of each row. Add one row of dark blue beads inside the pink rows.

FINAL LAYOUT

Figure 3-9

Now, draw the four directions or cross pattern in the center of the rosette. To do this, first take a compass and draw a small circle, about 5/16 inch in diameter, in the center of the rosette. Then, select a point on the edge of the last row of dark blue beads and make a small dot there (point A in Figure 3-8). Align a ruler through this dot and the center dot, and make a mark on the opposite side of the dark blue circle (point B). Draw a line between the marks, skipping the

⊙ *Transparent Pink*   ● *Dark Blue*

○ *White*   ⊖ *Lt Blue*   ⊕ *Lavender*

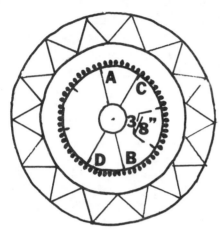

Figure 3-8

small circle in the center.

Make another mark 3/8 inch from the first one (point C), and using the center dot as a reference, draw a second line across the dark blue circle, once again skipping the center circle (line C-D in Figure 3-8). Draw two more lines at 3/8 inch intervals, dividing the area within the circle of dark blue beads into eight equal sections.

FINAL BEADING

Because of the small area remaining and the tightness of the curves, switch to a Two Bead Return Stitch for the rest of the rosette. Begin just inside the circle of dark blue beads at one of the lines just drawn. Use one dark blue bead and one white bead in the first stitch and position the dark blue bead directly on top of the guideline. Stitch on enough white beads to reach the next guideline, add a dark blue bead directly on this next line, and then continue on with white beads. Follow this pattern of white and dark blue around the circle to the end of the row (Figure 3-9).

Working inward, bead the next row with

sections of lavender and light blue between the lines, putting dark blue spacers on the guidelines between these two colors (see Figure 3-9). With the first stitch, place one dark blue bead on the guideline and either a lavender or light blue bead next to it. Stitch the same color beads over to the next guideline, put a dark blue bead on the line, then bead the next section in the second color. Continue in this manner until the row is completed.

Continue beading rows in towards the inner 5/16 inch circle using the same color scheme as the previous row; that is, lavender and light blue sections divided by dark blue lines. This should require about three more rows.

When the center circle is reached, finish the work with rows of transparent pink beads. There should be room for two rows worked around the circle and a single transparent pink bead in the center of the piece. Secure the thread with a Backstitch Knot hidden in the rows of beadwork.

CONSTRUCTION AND EDGING

With the beadwork finished on the rosettes, it is now time to sew the pieces of the hair ties together. First remove the masking tape from the backs of the beaded pieces, then trim the unbeaded edges of the buckskin to about 1/8

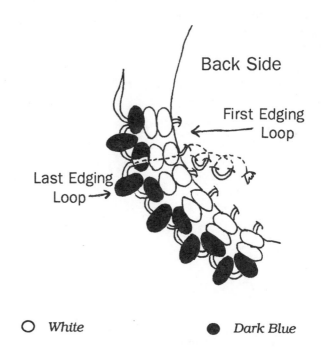

○ *White*   ● *Dark Blue*

inch from the edge of the beadwork (Figure 3-10).

    Trim one piece of blank buckskin and one piece of cowhide to match each of the beaded pieces. Cut the cowhide pieces slightly smaller than the buckskin ones. Place each cowhide disc between a beaded rosette and a blank piece of buckskin (flesh side in) and Whipstitch the two pieces of buckskin together around the cowhide (Figure 3-11). Secure the thread with a Backstitch Knot on the back of the piece.

    Finish the edge of each rosette with a Loop Edging Stitch. The color sequence for the first loop is as follows: two white, three dark blue, and two white beads. Squeeze the middle dark blue bead to the top of the stitch. For the second loop, string two dark blue beads and two white beads on the thread and take another small stitch, squeezing the first dark blue bead to the top of the stitch. Continue around the rosette until the edge is completely beaded (Figure 3-12). For the last loop, add a single dark blue bead, then pass the thread through the first three beads of the first loop. Secure the thread with a Backstitch Knot on the back of the piece.

    Now add a beaded fringe to the bottom third of each rosette. Start with a Backstitch Knot on the back of the piece, on either side of the rosette about a third of the way up from the bottom. Run the thread to the edge of the beading by passing it through the beads in one of the edging loops and exiting through the dark blue bead at the center of the loop. String the first set of fringe beads on the thread. The color sequence for each fringe is as follows: seven transparent pink, seven lavender, seven light blue, and one dark blue. Bring the thread back through all the fringe beads except the last one. Finally, run the thread through the center bead of the next edging loop towards the bottom of the hair tie (Figure 3-13). Add the beads for the next fringe to the

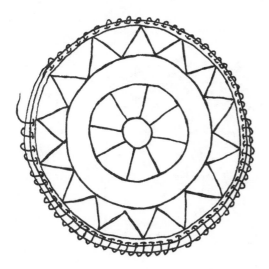

Figure 3-11

thread.

Continue adding fringes in the same manner until the bottom third of the rosette is fringed. There should be about 24 fringes. To end, pass the thread through several more of the dark blue edging beads. Then take the thread down to the leather through a set of loop edge beads, as was done to start the fringe. Tie off the thread with a Backstitch Knot on the back of the leather.

Finally, add the ties to the rosettes. Punch two holes in the center of each back piece of buckskin with an awl. Take care not to go through the cowhide blank. Push one of the buckskin thongs through both holes on the back of each rosette (Figure 3-14) and center the rosettes on the thongs.

Figure 3-13

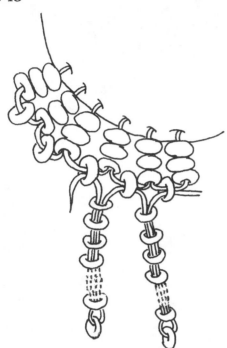

Figure 3-14

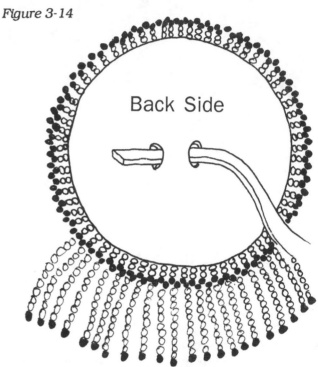

26

RATION TICKET BAG

Materials
2   Buckskin Pieces - 6" x 8"
2   Wine Red Velvet Pieces - 6" x 8"
2   Cotton Muslin Pieces - 6" x 8"
1   Buckskin Strip - 2 1/2" x 5"
1   Buckskin Welt Strip - 1/4" x 12"
1   Small Spool White Silk Thread - Size A
2   Snap Fasteners
1   Light Blue Tailor's Chalk Pencil
7   Hanks 12/° Seed Beads:
1 Rose Pink, 1 Transparent Dark Green,
1 Greasy Yellow, 1 Transparent Medium Blue,
1 Transparent Light Blue, 1 White, & 1 Lavender

This is a nice old time piece. The pattern, colors and materials are widely popular and very traditional, right down to the use of silk thread. The snaps, of course, are a modern adaptation. The bag can be worn on a belt at the side or in the front, but it was most often placed over the belt ties in the back. The name is derived from the original use of the bag, which was to hold valuable ration tickets during earlier reservation times.

INITIAL CONSTRUCTION

The pattern for this bag is provided on a grid in Figure 4-1 where one square is equal to one square inch. The back of the bag is cut using the entire pattern, while the front of the bag is cut only as high as the dotted line running across the pattern about three quarters of the way up from the bottom. Cut one front and one back each from the leather (buckskin), the velvet, and the cotton muslin.

Place each piece of velvet on the grain side of the matching piece of leather and, stitching as close to the edge as possible, baste the velvet to the leather with a fairly large Running Stitch (Figure 4-2). This stitching must be close to the edge so that it can be covered later by the edge beading.

BEADING INSTRUCTIONS

Do the beading for this project on the smaller front piece of velvet. The leather provides a firm backing for beading and later helps maintain the bag's shape and tidy appearance.

This design provides an excellent opportunity to use the Three Bead and Two Bead Return Stitches, changing from one to the other as the beading conditions change. Use a Three Bead Return Stitch in the longer, straighter lines and the Two Bead Return variation on the tighter curves in the beadwork. Stitch only through the velvet and secure the thread with a Backstitch Knot where necessary. Sections that are side by side can be worked with continuous stitching rather than stopping to knot the thread between sections. Notice while beading this pattern, that the direction in which the rows are applied always reinforces the shape of that element of the design.

The beading pattern is drawn on the velvet

Figure 4-1

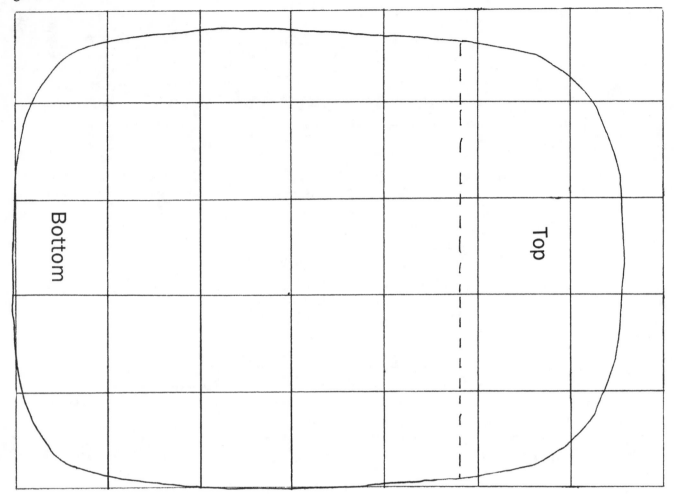

Bottom

Top

Leather Backing

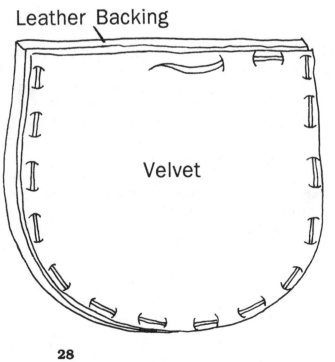

Velvet

Figure 4-2

28

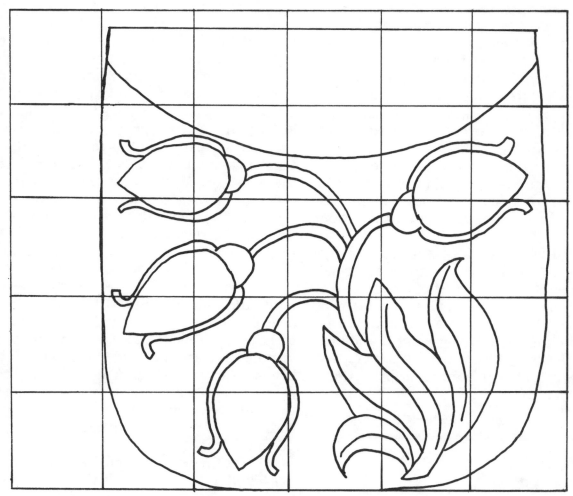

Figure 4-3

g   *Transparent Dark Green*

p   *Rose Pink*

w   *White*

mb   *Transparent Medium Blue*

lb   *Transparent Light Blue*

l   *Lavender*

ooo   *Greasy Yellow*

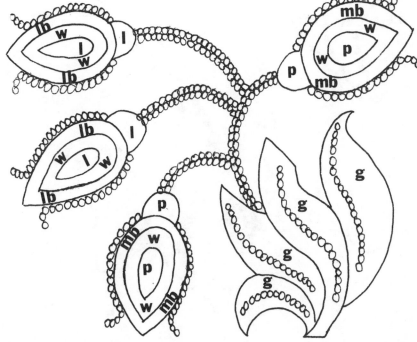

Figure 4-4

29

freehand with a tailor's chalk pencil. This is a good piece to practice freehand drawing as the tailor's chalk brushes off the velvet quite easily if an error is made. Small sections are drawn and then beaded right away for this same reason.

The pattern for the design is drawn full size on a grid in Figure 4-3 and should be easy to follow. A color-keyed diagram of the design is provided in Figure 4-4; refer to it as needed while beading.·

Draw the two leaves on the extreme right side of the design first. Position this first section carefully, leaving about 1/4 inch between the leaves and the edges of the bag for the beaded border.

Start the beadwork by outlining the first two leaves with transparent dark green beads and a Three Bead Return Stitch (Figure 4-5). Begin at the bottom of the first leaf at point A and bead up the right side to the top at point B. Take a small stitch in the velvet at point B and bead down the left side of the leaf, back to point A. Next outline the second leaf, starting at point C and

beading up to point D. Again take a small stitch at point D, then bead down the outside of the leaf to point E.

Fill these leaves with vertical rows of beads which follow the contours of the outlining rows. Again, start at point A and bead the first row with dark green to the top of the leaf (Figure 4-6). Take a small stitch and bead back to the bottom of the leaf, again with dark green. The third row runs from bottom to top, but this row is partially made up of greasy yellow beads, which form a vein in the leaf. Start the row with five or six dark green beads, switch to greasy yellow along the vein, then end the row with two or three dark green beads. The remainder of the leaf is filled with rows of dark green beads which run up and down the leaf.

Work the second leaf in this section in much the same manner. Begin at point E and bead the first row with dark green beads to the top of the leaf. In this leaf, the second row depicts the vein and is partially beaded with greasy yellow beads. Start with two dark green beads at the top of the leaf, switch to greasy yellow, and end with two dark green beads. The rest of the leaf is filled with rows of dark green beads worked up and down the leaf.

For the next section, draw in leaves number 3 and 4, to the left of leaves 1 and 2. Bead these two leaves in the same manner as the previous two with one exception; bead leaf 3 horizontally from the top row towards the bottom row, without a bottom outline (Figure 4-7). Outline the top of leaf 3 first with dark green beads;

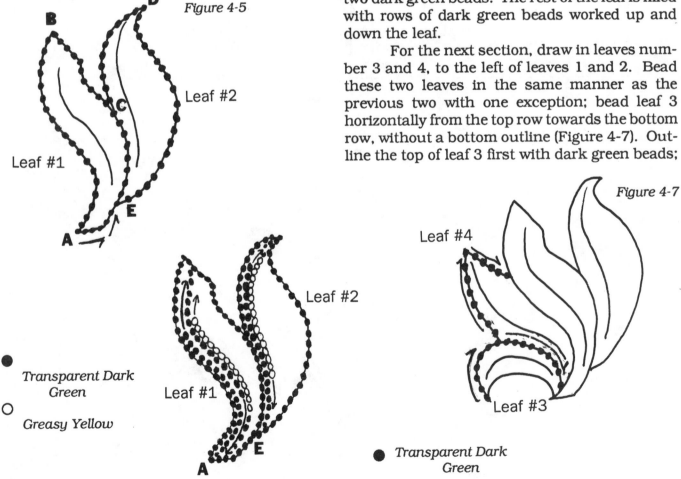

Figure 4-5

Leaf #2

Leaf #1

D

B

C

E

A

● Transparent Dark
Green

○ Greasy Yellow

Figure 4-6

Leaf #2

Leaf #1

E

A

Figure 4-7

Leaf #4

Leaf #3

● Transparent Dark
Green

30

Figure 4-8

Leaf #4

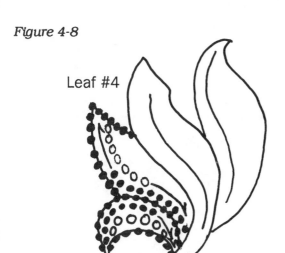

Leaf #3

● *Transparent Dark Green*
○ *Greasy Yellow*

then bead up the left side of leaf 4, take a small stitch, and finish outlining down the right side of this leaf.

Fill leaf 3 with a Two Bead Return Stitch because of the tight curve. Add a second row of dark green, then a row of greasy yellow (Figure 4-8). Finish with rows of dark green. Fill leaf 4 from left to right, returning to a Three Bead Return

Figure 4-9

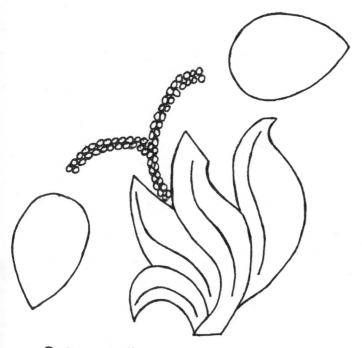

○ *Greasy Yellow*

Stitch. Again, add a row of dark green, then a row of greasy yellow. Fill the remainder of the leaf with rows of dark green which run up and down the leaf.

Draw the main flower stem, which leads to the flower bud on the right. Bead it with two rows of greasy yellow beads and a Three Bead Return Stitch (Figure 4-9). Then draw the stem that leads to the bottom bud on the left and bead it with two rows of greasy yellow beads. Finally, draw the two flower buds that go with the stems just beaded. Place them about 1/4 inch away from the stems, leaving room for the small half circles which go between the stems and the buds.

Bead the two buds just drawn with the same color sequence. Start with an outline of transparent medium blue beads. Begin at the tip of each bud and bead all the way around the guideline until the tip is reached again. Take a small stitch in the velvet so that the thread emerges exactly where the next row should start (Figure 4-10). This technique places the rows so that each follows the shape of the bud, enhancing this portion of the design.

Point of Flower Bud

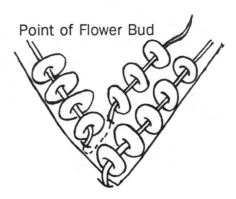

Figure 4-10

Bead a second row of medium blue beads inside of the outline, as shown in the lower bud in Figure 4-11. Continue beading inward with two rows of white beads. Work from the tip and go around the bud until the tip is reached again, as shown in the upper bud in Figure 4-11. Fill the rest of the bud with rows of rose pink beads which run in the same direction as the previous ones. Switch to a Two Bead Return Stitch for more control when the curve gets tight. The number of rows will vary according to the exact size of the buds.

31

Figure 4-11   Figure 4-12

● Medium Blue
○ White
◑ Greasy Yellow

○ Greasy Yellow

● Pink

When both buds are beaded, draw the two small half circles that connect these buds to the stems. Outline these half circles with a Two Bead Return Stitch. Start at one edge of the bud outline (point A in Figure 4-12) and bead with rose pink around the curved portion of the semi-circle to point B. Continue adding rows of rose pink beads, beading back and forth inside the semi-circular outline until the area is filled.

To finish these buds, draw the small re-curved petal lines that outline the two buds (see Figure 4-3). Bead each of them with one row of greasy yellow beads, returning to the use of a Three Bead Return Stitch.

Next, draw the last two stems on the top left side. Bead them as the others, with two rows of greasy yellow beads.

Draw the buds that go with these stems. Bead them in the same manner as the other two buds, using transparent light blue for the two outside rows. Add two rows of white beads inside the blue and then fill the center with rows of lavender beads. Once again, the number of lavender rows will vary according to the size the buds were actually drawn.

Draw the small half circles between the stems and the buds and bead them with lavender

beads in the same manner as the previous two half circles.

Finally, draw the recurved lines which outline these buds and bead each of them with one row of greasy yellow beads. This finishes the floral design of the bag. Before any more beading can be done, the bag must be sewn together.

FINAL CONSTRUCTION

Sew the belt loop on the velvet side of the back (unbeaded) piece of the bag. Begin by rounding the corners of the 2 1/2 by 5 inch strip of buckskin which will form the belt loop. The top portion of the back piece (above the dotted line in the pattern) is the flap which folds over the front of the bag and closes it. Fold this flap over, as it will be when the bag is finished. Place the belt loop on the back of the bag, upside down, with the bottom about 1 inch below the fold and center it from side to side (Figure 4-13).

Use a Running Stitch and the silk thread and beading needle to sew the top of the belt loop, still upside down, to the top of the bag. Stitch in an elongated oval around the end of the belt loop, then fill in the gaps between stitches by stitching around a second time. Keep the stitches small for

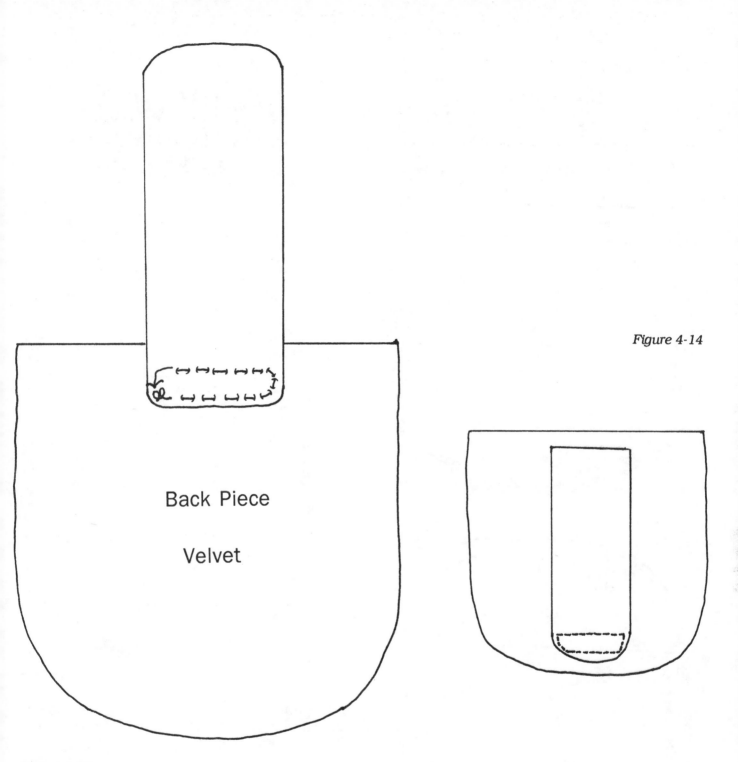

Figure 4-14

Back Piece

Velvet

Figure 4-13

a strong, tight seam. Fold the belt loop down over the seam and stitch the bottom of the loop to the bottom of the bag in an elongated oval, as was done at the top (Figure 4-14). This bottom seam will remain exposed. Keep the stitches small and sew around the oval twice.

Add the cotton muslin lining next. Use a Running Stitch to baste the front and back muslin pieces to the leather sides of the front and back of the bag. Stitch around the outside, as close to the edge as possible, in the same fashion as the velvet was sewn to the leather.

With this done, the bag is ready to be sewn together. Place the front and back pieces together with the velvet sides facing out. Put the 1/4 inch buckskin welt between the two pieces of the bag around the outside edge. Whipstitch through the welt and both pieces of the bag. Start at the top

Figure 4-15

Figure 4-17

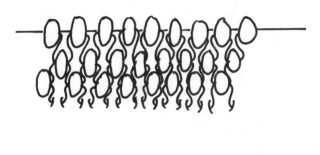

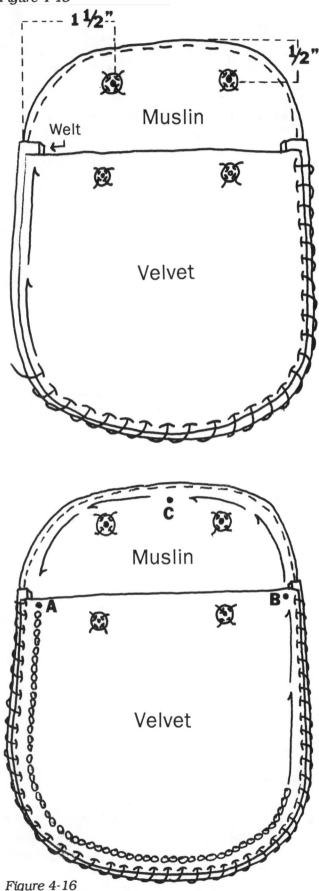

1 ½"

½"

Welt

Muslin

Velvet

Figure 4-16

Muslin

C

A

B

Velvet

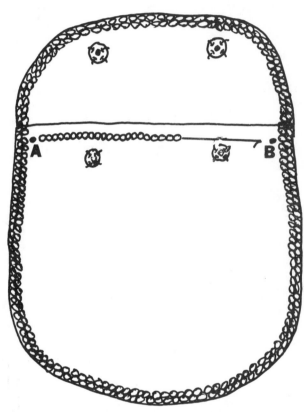

A

B

Figure 4-18

of the front piece of the bag on either side and sew down and around to the top of the front on the other side (Figure 4-15).

Finish the construction of the bag by sewing the snaps in place. Sew the male halves of the snaps to the muslin side of the top flap first. Position them 1 1/2 inches in from the sides and 1/2 inch down from the edge of the flap (see Figure 4-15). Sew through the muslin and partially through the leather, stitching through each hole in the snap several times for a secure fastening. Hide the knots under the edges of the snaps.

Mark the correct positions for the female halves of the snaps by folding the flap down over the top edge of the bag and pressing firmly. Mark the snap impressions on the bag with a tailor's chalk pencil. Make sure the marks are low enough to allow 1/2 inch for the beaded edging at the top of the front piece. If the marks are too close to the edge, it should be possible to lower their placement slightly without affecting the fit of the top flap. Sew the female halves of the snaps on these marks in the same way as the male halves were sewn (see Figure 4-15).

BEADED EDGING

Edge this bag with a Gourd Stitch Edging and rose pink beads. Sew the first row of the edging around the front of the bag with a Two Bead Return Stitch, about 1/4 inch from the edge (Figure 4-16). Begin in the upper left corner (point A) and work down and around the bottom, then back up to the upper right corner (point B). Continue up onto the flap, to point C and then on around the top edge of the flap back to point A. The section on the flap is worked on the muslin, on the inside of the flap.

Work subsequent rows in the network style of the Gourd Stitch and run them completely around the bag. There will be no need to take stitches between rows as they are oval. Add enough rows to the beadwork so that the stitching on the back of the bag will be covered when the edging is stitched down to the velvet. When the final row is completed, fold the beadwork tightly over the seam. To stitch the final row to the back of the bag, pass the thread through the last bead in the row, then through the velvet and partially through the leather. Go through the next bead, then back through the velvet. Stitch each bead in this row to the velvet in this manner to hold the edging firmly in place (Figure 4-17). Secure the end of the thread with a Backstitch Knot.

Finally, add a Gourd Stitch edging across the top edge of the front of the bag (Figure 4-18). Begin about 1/4 inch down from the top, on the left edge of the bag (point A), with a row of Two Bead Return Stitch; work across the top edge to point B. Once again, use rose pink beads. Add subsequent rows in the net form of this stitch until there are enough rows in the edging to fold over the top edge of the bag and cover the stitching on the inside. Stitch the last row down on the inside of the bag, in the same manner as the edging around the outside of the bag was done.

STRIKE-A-LIGHT BAG

Materials	
2	Buckskin or Thin Cowhide Pieces - 6" x 4"
1	Buckskin or Thin Cowhide Piece - 3" x 4"
1	Buckskin Thong - 18" long
2	Buckskin Welt Strips - 1/4" x 5 3/8"
20	Tin Cones
1	Bobbin Nymo Beading Thread - Size A
1	Pair Needle Nosed Pliers
5	Hanks Size 12/° Seed Beads:
	1 White, 1 Mustard Yellow, 1 Transparent Dark Blue,
	1 Brick Red, & 1 Medium "Pony Trader" Blue

The term Strike-A-Light refers to the use of this item in days long past. At one time nearly everyone carried the means for starting a fire on their person at all times. Flint, steel, and tinder were most often carried together and this style bag was a favorite method of carrying them on a belt. The beadwork design is a common Central Plains motif.

LAYOUT

The pattern for this bag is provided on a grid in Figure 5-1 where one square is equal to one square inch. The back of the bag is cut using the entire pattern, while the front is cut only as high as the dotted line running across the 5th row of squares from the bottom. This dotted line designates where the back piece is folded down to form a flap which closes the bag.

Cut one front and one back from the 6 x 4 inch pieces of buckskin. Also cut the welts at this time; cut two strips of buckskin which are 1/4 inch wide and the length of the front piece of the bag from the leftover scrap pieces.

Put strips of masking tape on the flesh side of the front piece of the bag to maintain a firm drawing and beading surface.

Begin laying out the beading pattern on the front piece of the bag, drawing on the grain side of the leather. Draw border lines 1/4 inch from the side and bottom edges of the buckskin and then draw a top border line 3/8 inch down from the top edge (Figure 5-2). Use a ruler and pen to draw the lines; straight lines are essential to a linear pattern such as this one.

Divide the area inside these border lines into horizontal quarters. To do this, first mark the midpoint of each side border, then divide the area in half by drawing a line between the marks (line 3 in Figure 5-2). Divide the two areas created by this line in half again to complete the quarters (lines 2 and 4). These lines do not mark beadwork areas; they are guides for determining the accurate placement of the design lines. They are also used to keep the rows of beadwork straight across the bag, combating the tendency to angle up or down. The lines are numbered 1 through 5, from bottom to top, for the purpose of describing how the design is drawn.

Still using Figure 5-2 as a guide, mark the reference points for drawing the hourglass designs, which consist of a series of diamonds on top of one another. First find the exact center of line 3 and mark it (point A). Do the same with lines 1 (point B) and 5 (point C). Check with a

Figure 5-1

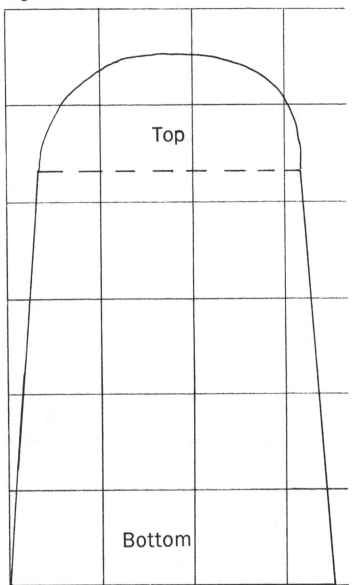

Figure 5-2

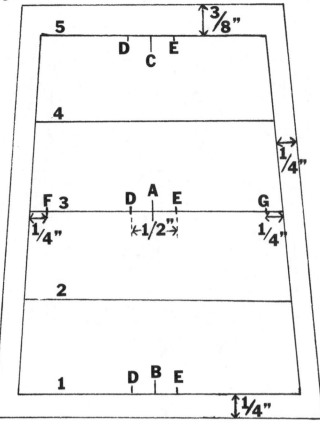

straight edge, such as a good metal ruler, to see that all three marks line up vertically.

Next make small marks, 1/4 inch to either side of these center marks (points D and E on each line).

Now make two small marks on the center line (line 3), 1/4 inch from each side border (points F and G).

Complete the diamonds of the hourglass design, by drawing four large X's within the border guidelines. The first line of each X is shown as a solid line in Figure 5-3 and the second line is shown as a dotted line.

Begin at point F on line 3, and use the ruler to draw a line from this point to point D on line 5. Next draw a line from point D on line 3 up to the top left corner, crossing line F-D exactly at line

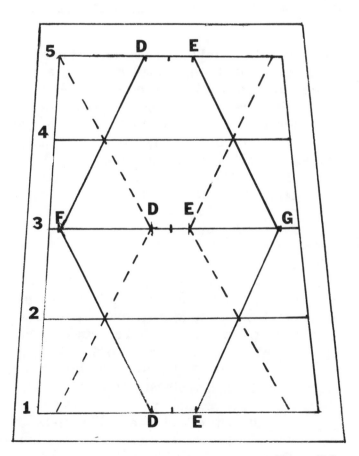

Figure 5-3

37

Figure 5-4   Figure 5-5

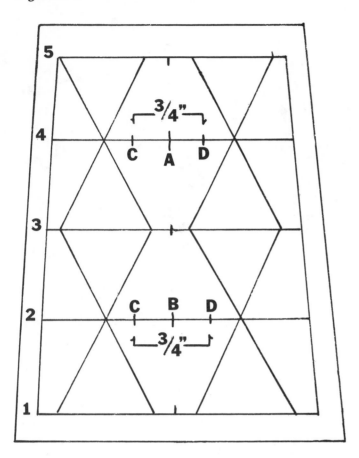

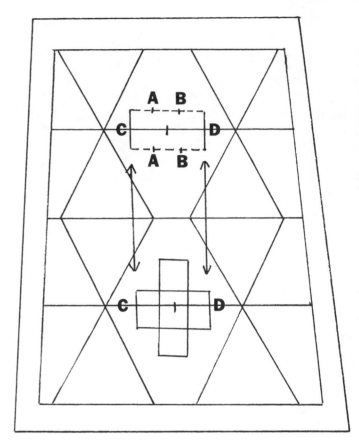

four. The end point of this second line need not be precisely in the upper left corner; it can be moved to accommodate the crossing at line 4.

Next draw a line from point G on line 3 to point E on line 5. The second half of this X goes from point E on line 3 to the upper right corner, crossing line E-G exactly at line 4.

Draw the next line from point F on line 3 to point D on line 1. The second half of this X goes from point D on line 3 towards the lower left corner, crossing line D-F exactly at line 2. The end point of this line is determined by the crossing at line two.

The final X is drawn from point G on line 3 to point E on line 1. The second line of this X goes from point E on line 3 down towards the lower right corner, crossing line E-G exactly at line 2.

The next step is to draw two four directions designs (crosses) at the top and bottom of the bag. Each design consists of two rectangles drawn at right angles to one another.

Using Figure 5-4 as a guide, mark the reference points for the horizontal rectangles first. Find the center of lines 4 (point A) and 2 (point B) and mark these points. Check with a ruler to make sure these marks line up with the center marks on the other lines. Then place two marks on each of these lines, 3/8 inch to either side of the center marks (points C and D). These marks denote the ends of the horizontal rectangles.

Align a ruler between point C on line 2 and point C on line 4 as shown by the arrows in Figure 5-5. Draw two vertical lines, 3/8 inch in length, centered on lines 2 and 4. These lines should extend 3/16 inch above lines 2 and 4 and 3/16 inch below them. Repeat this procedure at the two point D's. Complete both horizontal rectangles by connecting the tops and then the bottoms of the vertical lines just drawn.

Begin the vertical portions of the four directions designs by dividing the horizontal rectangles into thirds. Make small marks 1/4 inch apart (points A and B in Figures 5-5 and 5-6) on the top and bottom lines (lines E and F) of each rectangle.

Align a ruler on two of these marks (A-A or B-B) and draw a vertical line 1 inch long, centered on line 4 (Figure 5-7). Do the same on the other side, then complete the rectangle by joining these vertical lines at the top and the bottom (see Figure 5-5).

Use the color-keyed diagram in Figure 5-8 as a guide and draw the lines which divide each central diamond into five differently colored areas. These lines are approximately 3/8 and 5/8 inch from both the top and bottom points of the diamonds. They are approximate guidelines which remind the beader of necessary color changes and also serve as aids in keeping the rows of beadwork straight.

Finally, draw the two small triangles in the center of each of these diamonds and the small vertical rectangles in the centers of the four directions designs (see Figure 5-8). Again these are approximate reminders and the exact locations may vary with bead and row placement.

Wait until the front and back of the bag are

Figure 5-6

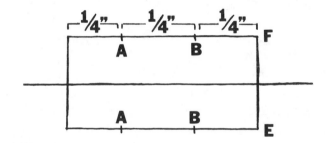

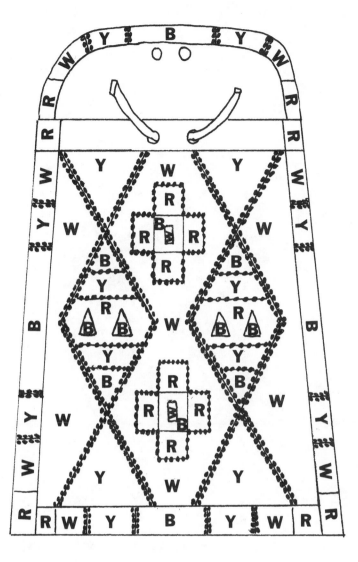

●   *Transparent Dark Blue*
Y   *Mustard Yellow*
R   *Red Whitehearts*
B   *Pony Trader Blue*
W   *White*

Figure 5-8

sewn together to mark the color changes in the border.

INITIAL BEADING

Start the beadwork inside the 1/4 inch border, in the lower left corner of the bag (point A in Figure 5-9). Use a Three Bead Return Stitch and bead the first row along the bottom guideline to the lower right corner (point B). Bead the background with white beads, place two dark

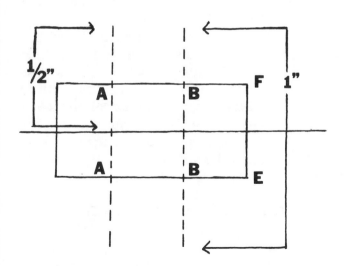

Figure 5-7

39

blue beads on either side of each hourglass guideline, and use yellow beads inside the hourglass designs. Follow the design guidelines closely when making color changes and consult the color

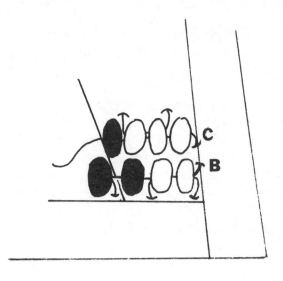

Figure 5-10

Figure 5-9

○ White
● Dark Blue
◉ Yellow

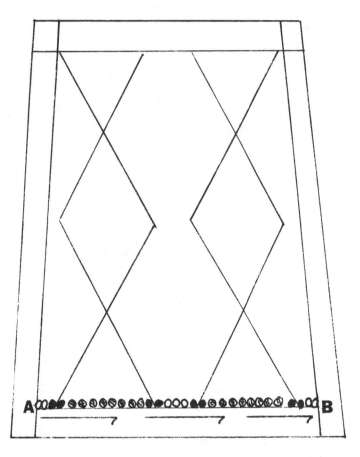

key in Figure 5-8.

When the end of the first row is reached, take a small stitch in the leather at point B (Figure 5-10), positioning the thread to start a second row immediately above the first at point C. Bead the second row from the right side of the bag towards the left. Turn the leather upside down to bead in this direction. The color scheme in this row is the same relative to the guidelines.

Continue working back and forth inside the border in this manner. Follow the color scheme in Figure 5-8 closely and pay attention to transitions in bead colors to maintain crisp definition of the pattern.

Any slight deviation from the guidelines in

this section of the beadwork will result in bigger and bigger problems as the work progresses. To avoid this, stretch or crowd the beads in a stitch as needed to maintain the integrity of the pattern. Stretching and crowding are controlled by the length of the stitch taken on the leather and by the position of the return stitch, which helps in spacing the beads evenly. When crowding, if one or more of the beads bunches up the stitch or forms a lump in the beadwork, pull the stitch out and use a long Two Bead Return Stitch instead. This will stretch two beads over a larger than usual space and while it may seem noticeable at first, small variations in spacing will not show when the beadwork is completed. A lump in the beads or a wobble in the color design, however, will show to great disadvantage in a finished piece and should be avoided at all costs.

Complete the beadwork inside the border area, still using a Three Bead Return Stitch. Continue the double dark blue outline of the hourglass design. Put a single dark blue outline on the outside guidelines of the four directions designs and on the horizontal guidelines within the central diamonds. Don't forget the color changes within these design elements, especially the small white rectangles inside the four directions designs and the small blue triangles inside the central diamonds.

INITIAL CONSTRUCTION

Sew the bag together before beading the borders. The seam will be covered with beadwork, so the bag can be sewn together right side out.

Put the front and back pieces together, with the beaded side of the front and the grain side of the back piece facing out. Insert the 3 x 4 inch piece of buckskin in the bottom seam, with the grain side facing towards the front. Stitch across the bottom of the bag with a Running Stitch and the needle and thread used for the beading. Go

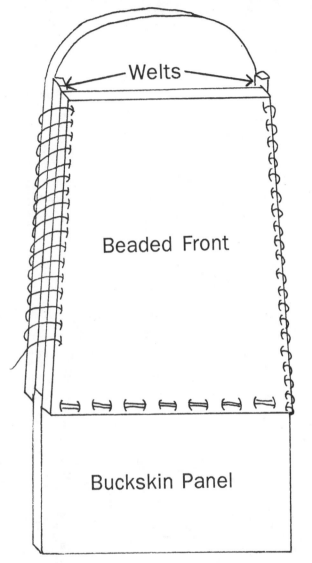

Figure 5-11

through all three thicknesses of leather to close the bottom of the bag (Figure 5-11). The bottom panel will act as a welt in the seam, protecting the thread from wear on the inside of the bag. This piece of buckskin will be cut into the fringe on the bottom of the bag.

Place the 1/4 inch wide leather welts between the front and back pieces on the side edges. Put them in the seam above the bottom panel, so that the side and bottom welts do not overlap (see Figure 5-11). Stitch the side seams together with

a closely spaced Whip Stitch, going through all three thicknesses of leather.

FINAL BEADING

Once the bag is sewn together, layout the color changes in the border areas. First, draw a 3/8 inch border around the edge of the top flap to serve as a guideline for this beaded edge. Draw the line on the grain side of the leather (when the flap is up, this is on the back of the bag; when the flap is folded down, this line will be on the front of the bag). Using Figure 5-8 as a guide, mark the various color changes on the side and flap borders. Because of variations in bead and stitch width, it may not be possible to follow these color change marks exactly. Their exact location is not critical but do use them as guides and reminders.

Once the border is clearly marked, bead the side edges with a Lazy Stitch seam cover. Start at the top of either side on the front of the bag. Put enough beads on the thread to cover both the border and the stitching on the back of the bag. This should take about ten or eleven beads. Lay the beads around the seam, and take a small stitch on the back. Add the same number of beads for the second row, lay them around the edge to the front of the bag and take another stitch.

Repeat this sequence, back and forth, down the side of the bag. Follow the color chart in Figure 5-8 and make sure there are enough beads in each stitch to wrap around the sides entirely and cover the stitching on the back of the bag. The different colors of beads may vary in size, so check the number of beads at each color change. It may be necessary to add or subtract from the original number according to color. When the bottom of the bag is reached, tie off the thread and repeat this procedure on the opposite side of the bag.

Bead the bottom border with a Three Bead Return Stitch. Again, follow the color sequence in Figure 5-8. Bead the first row along the top edge of the border, just below the main design. Bead in horizontal rows from the top of the border down towards the bottom of the bag (Figure 5-12). Do just enough rows to cover the stitching in the bottom seam of the bag; three or four rows will probably be enough.

Begin the edging on the top flap with a single row of white beads along the guideline

41

Figure 5-12

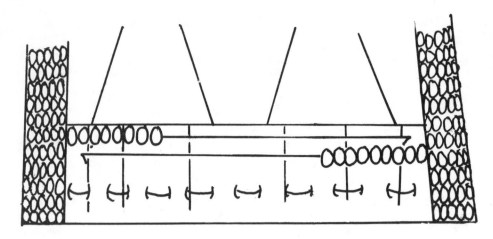

(Figure 5-13); use a Three Bead Return Stitch. Finish the border of the flap with a Lazy Stitch; use seven or eight beads for each stitch and wrap the beadwork around the edge of the flap to the inside. Again, use Figure 5-8 and the marks drawn on the border to determine the correct color sequence.

FINAL CONSTRUCTION

All that remains to be done are the fringe and tin cones on the bottom of the bag, the ties which close the flap, and the belt loop.

First, cut the bottom panel of buckskin into twenty fringes. Taper the bottom of each fringe to a point, then dampen and twist them into sharper points to make it easier to push the cones onto the fringes. Thread a tin cone onto each strand of fringe and push them nearly to the top of the strands, so that they almost touch the bag. Crimp the tops of the cones with a pair of pliers to hold them in place. Trim off any extra leather hanging out the bottom of the cones. Gently pull the leather down when cutting it, so that when it rebounds the end of the leather will not show at the bottom of the cone.

To add the flap ties, punch two holes in the center of the flap, just below the beaded border, with a leather punch (see Figure 5-13). Fold the flap down and mark the position of the holes on the top (unbeaded) edge of the bag. Punch two corresponding holes on these marks (see Figure 5-8).

Cut a 4 inch piece off the buckskin thong.

Taper the ends to a point, then moisten and twist them into a sharper point. Thread the tie through the holes in the top of the bag as shown in Figure 5-8. To close the bag, thread these ties through the corresponding holes in the flap. Pull the flap down and tie it shut.

To attach the belt loop, punch two holes in the back of the bag with a leather punch. The flap must be open for this step. Position them one above the other, just below the point where the flap folds over (see Figure 5-13). Take as much of the remaining piece of leather thong as desired and run it through these holes. Knot the ends together just below the bottom hole with an overhand knot.

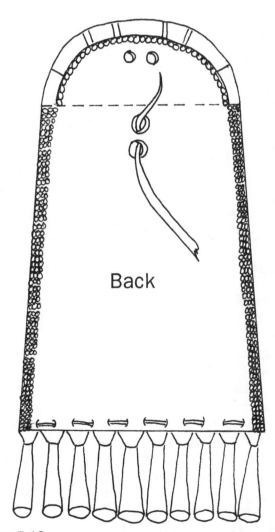

Back

Figure 5-13

ROUND FLORAL BELT BUCKLE

Materials
2   Round Buckskin Pieces - 4 1/2" diameter
1   Round Belt Buckle Blank - 4" diameter
1   Bobbin Nymo Beading Thread - Size A
1   Hank Size 12/° Cut Seed Beads: Light Green
5   Hanks Size 12/° Seed Beads:
1 Greasy Yellow, 1 White, 1 Transparent Dark Red,
1 Transparent Pink & 1 Transparent Dark Green

Belt buckles are always popular beaded items. The design for this particular buckle is an original adaptation of the Shoshone Rose pattern found so often in beadwork from the Intermountain West. As is true with most floral beadwork, in this design it is more important to fill a given area with beads gracefully than it is to create a precise copy of the original pattern. Although exact directions are given for the benefit of novice beadworkers, slight variations in size and shape are to be expected when recreating a piece like this one and such deviations should not be a cause for worry.

LAYOUT

Set aside one of the 4 1/2 inch buckskin circles to use as a liner on the back of the buckle blank. Put strips of masking tape on the back or grain side of the other buckskin circle.

Draw a 4 inch circle on this piece of leather, using a compass with a pencil marker. Make a small dot in the center of the circle with a marking pen and then trace the circle with the pen. This circle will mark the outside edge of the main design.

Next, draw a 3 inch circle inside of the previous one. This circle does not need to be gone over with a pen as it is only a guide for drawing the flower and need not be permanent.

Draw four lines across the circles, dividing them into five unequal parts (Figure 6-1). Since the lines are located unequal distances from the center of the circle, follow the measurements given carefully. Line A is 9/16 inch above the center mark and line B is 1 3/8 inches above the center mark. Line C is 5/16 inch below the center mark and line D is 1 1/8 inches below the center point. These lines aid in the correct placement of

the flower when it is drawn, and are also used to keep the rows horizontal and straight when the background is beaded.

Following the diagram in Figure 6-2, draw the flower and leaves onto the leather with a marking pen. Take careful note of where the petals and leaves cross the guidelines in the illustration; duplicating these crossings will make it much simpler to reproduce the pattern. Notice that the flower itself remains within the 3 inch circle. The flower petals in Figure 6-2 are numbered to simplify the beading instructions, as this project is beaded one petal at a time. It is not necessary to number the petals on the leather.

BEADING INSTRUCTIONS

A color-keyed diagram of the design is provided in Figure 6-3. It will be helpful to consult this diagram while beading.

Begin with a Three Bead Return Stitch and bead two rows of greasy yellow beads inside the 4 inch circle. This is the outside limit of the main

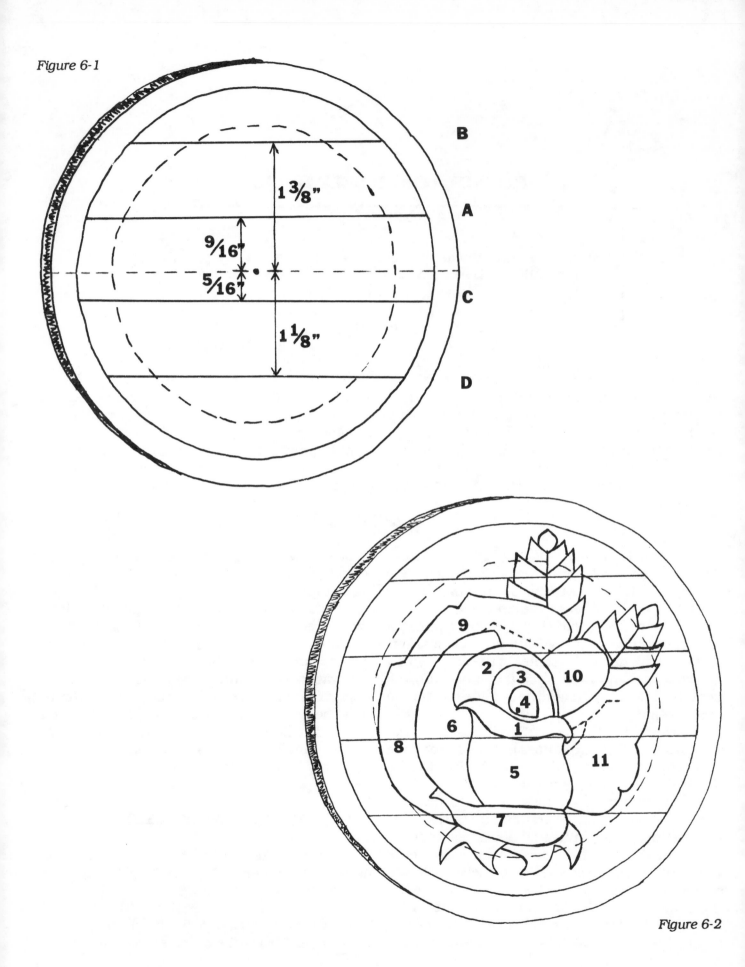

Figure 6-1

B

A

$1\frac{3}{8}"$

$\frac{9}{16}"$

$\frac{5}{16}"$

$1\frac{1}{8}"$

C

D

9

2   3   10

4

6   1

8

5   11

7

Figure 6-2

44

Figure 6-3

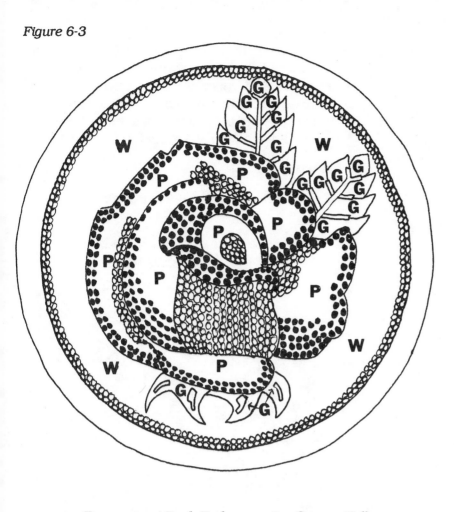

● Transparent Dark Red   ○ Greasy Yellow
◻ Light Green   G Trans Dk Green
P Transparent Pink   W White

design.

Bead the flower and leaf areas of the design with a Two Bead Return Stitch. The work in this area is too tight to use three beads at a time. The petals and leaves can be beaded with continuous rows, without knotting the thread. Just take a small stitch at the end of each row and emerge in the correct position to begin the next row. It may or may not be necessary to knot the thread between the different petals; this will depend upon the distance between the ending point of one petal and the beginning point of the next. More than one small stitch may be taken in the leather to get from one beading point to the next.

Start to bead the flower at petals number 1 and 2. Both these petals are beaded entirely in transparent dark red, one after the other. Figure 6-4 shows how the rows are worked in these petals.

Start petal 1 at the left tip (point A) and bead the first row of dark red beads along the bottom line to the right tip of the petal (point B). Take a small stitch in the leather and add a second row above the first, beading from point B back to point A. Fill the rest of the petal in the same manner, working back and forth with rows of dark red beads.

Petal 2 begins on the left outside edge, just above the starting point of petal 1 (point A). Bead the first row around the top of the petal until it meets petal 1 at point C. Work back and forth, following the first row, until the area of the petal is filled with rows of dark red beads.

Petals number 3 and 4 are also shown in Figure 6-4. Start petal 3 at the bottom right, near point C, and use transparent pink beads. Bead in a clockwise direction, all the way around the outside edge of this petal. When the beginning of the first row is reached again, take a small stitch sideways and start the second row just inside the first row. Bead in the opposite direction (counter-clockwise) around the top of the petal to where this row meets the first row on the left side of the petal (point D). Continue back and forth inside the top edge, filling the petal with rows of pink beads.

Bead petal 4 with greasy yellow beads.

Figure 6-4

● Trans Dk Red   ○ Trans Pink
◉ Greasy Yellow

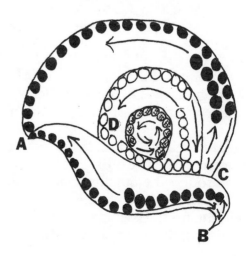

Start in the lower right portion of the petal and bead around the outer edge, then inward in a spiral until the space is filled.

Start petal number 5 in the upper right corner (point A in Figure 6-5). Bead down the right side with greasy yellow beads. When the bottom is reached, switch to transparent pink for the corner bead and bead one row of pink across the bottom of the petal. Begin the second row next to point A (point B) with greasy yellow beads and work inside the first row to the bottom of the petal. Start the third row at the bottom of the

remainder of the row. This row ends next to the first by point A. Following Figure 6-6, decrease the number of dark red beads in each row from left to right and increase the number of pink beads until the 5th row, which is entirely pink. Fill the rest of the petal with rows of pink beads.

Petal number 7 is located at the bottom of

Figure 6-6

● *Trans Dark Red*   ○ *Trans Pink*

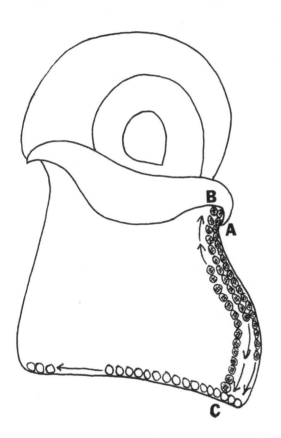

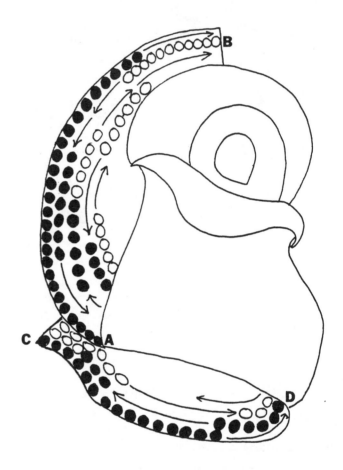

Figure 6-5

● *Trans Dk Red*   ○ *Trans Pink*
◉ *Greasy Yellow*

petal, inside the second at point C, and bead back up towards point B. Fill the remainder of the petal with rows of greasy yellow beads which run back and forth between the top of the petal and the bottom.

Petal number 6 starts in the bottom right corner at point A (Figure 6-6). Bead a row of dark red beads around the outside edge to the top at point B. Take a small stitch and start the second row inside the first. Use pink beads for the first half of this row, then switch to dark red for the

the flower and the beading sequence is shown in Figure 6-6. Begin the first row in the bottom left corner (point C). Use dark red beads and follow the bottom guideline to the far right side of the petal (point D). Begin the second row on the right side, next to the first, again using dark red beads. The last three beads in this second row are pink. Work back and forth, filling the remaining area in this petal with rows of pink beads.

Begin petals number 8 and 9 in the bottom right corner (point A in Figure 6-7). Use dark red beads and bead around the outside edge, following the guideline to the second tip at point B. The

46

second row is also entirely dark red; it starts at the third tip (point C) and goes back down to point A. Stay just inside the first row once point B is reached. Work the remainder of petal 8 only as far as the first tip (point D). Go back and forth inside the first rows with two rows of pink and then two rows of greasy yellow beads.

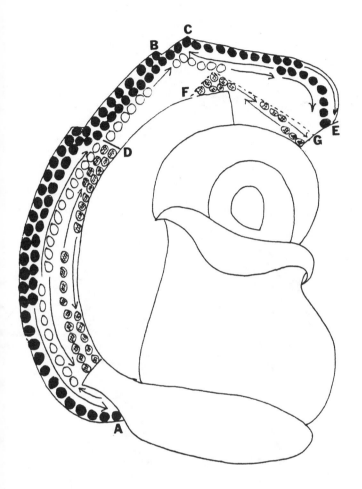

● T Dark Red   ○ Trans Pink   ◎ Greasy Yellow

Figure 6-7

Resume beading at point C in petal 9 (Figure 6-7) and bead around the top edge to point E with dark red beads. Run a second row of dark red, inside the first, from point E back to point C. Move to point F, where the dotted guideline intersects petal 6, and run a row of greasy yellow along the dotted line to point G. Fill this small area with greasy yellow beads, working back and forth as much as possible. This is a rather tight area and it may be necessary to add a single bead here and there to complete the fill.

Return to point D (Figure 6-7) and begin to fill the rest of petal 9 with pink beads. Work up

towards point C and then bead across the top from point C towards point E. Reverse direction and bead the next row back across the top, then down to point D again if possible. At some point, one of the pink rows will divide the remainder of petal 9 into two areas. Treat each area as a separate section from that point on and fill them by beading back and forth in the direction of the previous rows.

Start petal number 10 in the upper left corner (point A in Figure 6-8). Begin the first row with pink beads and work to the right; switch to dark red as soon as the beads draw even to the double row of dark red in the previous petal (petal 9). Continue the first row with dark red beads around the outside of petal 10, ending in the lower left corner (point B). Begin the second row beside the first, at point B, with dark red beads. Bead around the petal back to point A, switching to pink beads at the same place as in the first row. Fill the remainder of this petal with rows of pink beads, working back and forth around the petal inside the previous rows.

In petal number 11, begin the beadwork about two thirds of the way down the outside edge, at point C (Figure 6-8). Bead down to point D with dark red beads. Start the next row beside the first at point D. Bead up around the edge with dark red beads; go past point C to point F at the top of the petal and then over to point E. Note that this row goes to the outside edge of petal 11 once point C is passed. Begin the third row at point F and bead down to point D with dark red beads. Bead the 4th row inside the third; use dark red beads as far as point C, then switch to pink for the rest of the row. The next row, the 5th, follows the others and is pink except for four dark red beads at the end of the row by point G. Add a 6th row which is all pink beads.

Move to the top left corner of petal 11 (point H) and bead two rows of greasy yellow along the top edge. Take these rows past point E to the row of pink just added. The approximate location of this section is indicated by the dotted guideline extending across the petal from point H. This is just a guide however, and the actual width of the section should be determined by the space required for these two rows of beads (see Figure 6-8).

Next start a row of beadwork about two row widths below the tip of petal 1 (point I). Start with two pink beads, then switch to greasy yellow and

47

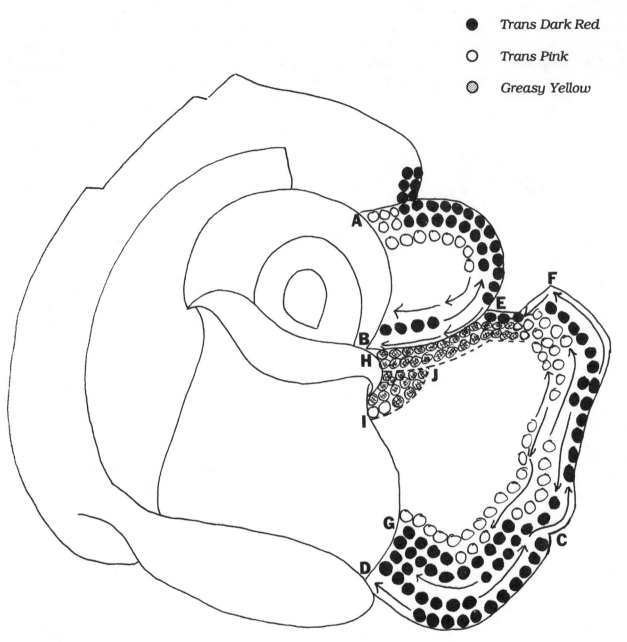

Figure 6-8

●   *Trans Dark Red*

○   *Trans Pink*

◉   *Greasy Yellow*

bead to point J, which is about a third of the way across the dotted line extending from point H (see Figure 6-8). Once again the approximate location of this section is indicated by a dotted guideline. While the color change in this section adds a great deal of visual interest to the design, the exact location is not critical and slight variations will not affect the beadwork in the remainder of the petal. Fill the rest of this small area with greasy yellow beads.

Return to point G and fill the remaining area in petal 11 with rows of pink beads. Work back and forth inside the previous rows running from point G to point E.

Bead the leaves next, still using a Two Bead Return Stitch. Start with the upper left leaf and begin beading at the bottom of the center vein (point A in Figure 6-9). Use light green cut seed beads and work from point A to the top of the vein at point B. Continue two beads past point B to the left, towards point C, and then finish the row from B to C with dark green beads. Next bead the right

Figure 6-9

O   *Light Green*

●   *Transparent Dark Green*

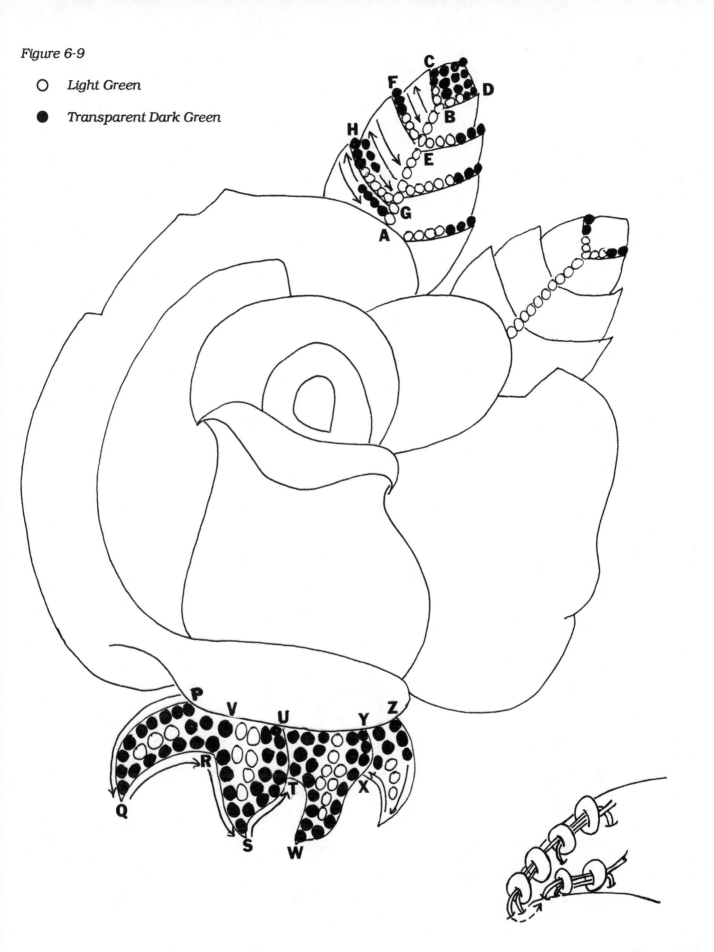

Figure 6-10

side vein from point B to point D with two light green beads and the rest dark green. Fill the small leaf tip with rows of dark green beads, following either B-C or B-D.

Move down to the second set of side veins at point E on the center vein (see Figure 6-9). Bead the left side vein towards point F, starting with three light green beads and finishing with dark green beads. Fill the area between E-F and B-C with rows of dark green beads.

Move down to the next set of side veins at point G on the center vein (see Figure 6-9). Work to the left towards point H, starting with five light green beads and finishing the row with dark green beads. Fill the area between G-H and E-F with rows of dark green beads, then fill the area under G-H with rows of dark green as well. Bead the other side of the leaf in the same manner. Repeat this whole procedure on the upper right leaf.

Start the bottom leaves in the upper left corner (point P in Figure 6-9). Use dark green beads and stitch around the outside edge of the left leaf. Bead down to the tip at point Q, then around past point R to the tip at point S, and finally up past point T to the base of the flower at point U. To maintain the sharp leaf points at Q and S, take a small stitch in the leather after the last bead on each point (Figure 6-10), then continue beading as described above. Put a second dark green row inside the first, from point U down to point S. Fill the rest of the area between U and V with two rows of light green cut beads. Finally, run a row of beads from point V to point Q; start with dark green beads, but switch to light green for the last three beads in this row.

Still following Figure 6-9, start the center bottom leaf at point T. Use dark green beads and run the first row from point T down to the tip at point W, then up past point X to the base of the flower at point Y. Begin a second row at point Y with two dark green beads. Switch to light green beads for the rest of the row, which runs down to point W. Place a third row, consisting entirely of light green beads, to the left of this second row. Fill the rest of the area between Y and U with dark green beads.

The final bottom leaf (on the right) starts at point Z with a row of dark green beads. Run this row down to the tip of the leaf, take a small stitch in the leather, then bead back up to point X. Start the next row to the left of point Z with two dark green beads, then bead down to the tip of the leaf with light green beads. Fill any remaining spaces with dark green beads.

Finish the area inside the 4 inch circle by filling the entire background with white beads. Begin on the left side (point A in Figure 6-11) and bead along the top horizontal guideline to its junction with the main design (point B). Fill the area above this line with rows of white beads, working back and forth between the yellow outline and the top leaf.

Return to point B and begin to fill the background area below the top guideline. Again, work back and forth between the yellow outline and the floral design. Keep an eye on the other guidelines, making sure that the rows remain horizontal. Stop at the tip of the first bottom leaf (point C).

Move to the right side of the design (point D) and bead a row along the bottom horizontal guideline to the yellow outline (point E). Fill the area beneath this line. When the tip of the last

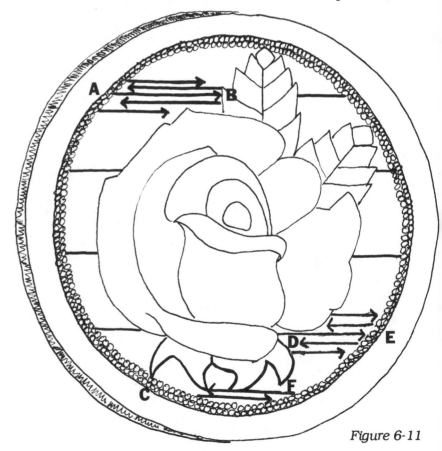

Figure 6-11

50

bottom leaf (point F) is reached, work the longest row possible in this area, then fill the remaining empty spaces on the bottom. This area is fairly tricky, so be careful to keep the rows horizontal. Return to point E and bead up the right side of the design, filling the rest of the background with horizontal rows of white beads.

CONSTRUCTION

Trim the edges of both pieces of buckskin (the beaded piece and the back liner) so that they are just slightly larger than the buckle blank. The buckskin pieces are sewn together around the blank, so let the thickness of the blank determine how much larger the buckskin pieces should be. Set the beaded piece aside.

Prepare the back piece of leather for placement on the blank by cutting two small slits for the belt loop (Figure 6-12). To place these cuts properly, first mark the center of the leather circle (point A). Place a ruler on the buckle blank and measure the distance from under the belt loop to the edge (x). Place the ruler on the leather from point A to the edge of the leather and make a mark which is this distance (x) from the edge (point B).

Now, measure the distance between the upright bars of the belt loop on the blank (y); the slits must be this distance apart. Place the ruler vertically on point B and make two marks which are distance y apart, with point B centered between them. The easiest way to do this is to place the halfway mark on the ruler at point B (e.g. put the 1 inch mark at point B if y is 2 inches) and then make the marks at 0 and y on the ruler (in the example the marks would be at 0 and 2 inches). These marks (points D and E) indicate the ends of the belt loop slits. Cut two slits, about 1/2 inch in length, from the edge of the leather to points D and E respectively (see Figure 6-12).

Next, punch a hole for the fastener. To position the hole, measure the distance of the fastener from the edge of the buckle blank (z). Lay the ruler across the leather, aligned with points A and B. Measure this distance (z) in from the far edge of the leather and make a mark (point C in Figure 6-12). Use a leather punch to make a hole at point C which will accommodate the fastener.

Place this piece of leather on the back of the buckle blank and stitch the slits closed around the belt loop bars with a small Whip Stitch (Figure 6-13).

Sew the front and back pieces of leather together, enclosing the buckle blank. Position the front piece so that the flower design will be in an upright position when the buckle is fastened. To ensure that the front piece remains upright and does not slide as the seam is stitched, tack it to the back piece with small temporary stitches in several places (see Figure 6-13). Any stitch and knot will do as the tacks are only temporary. Whip

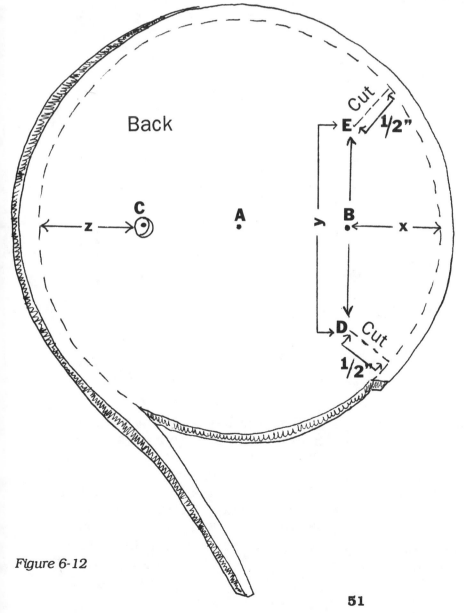

Figure 6-12

51

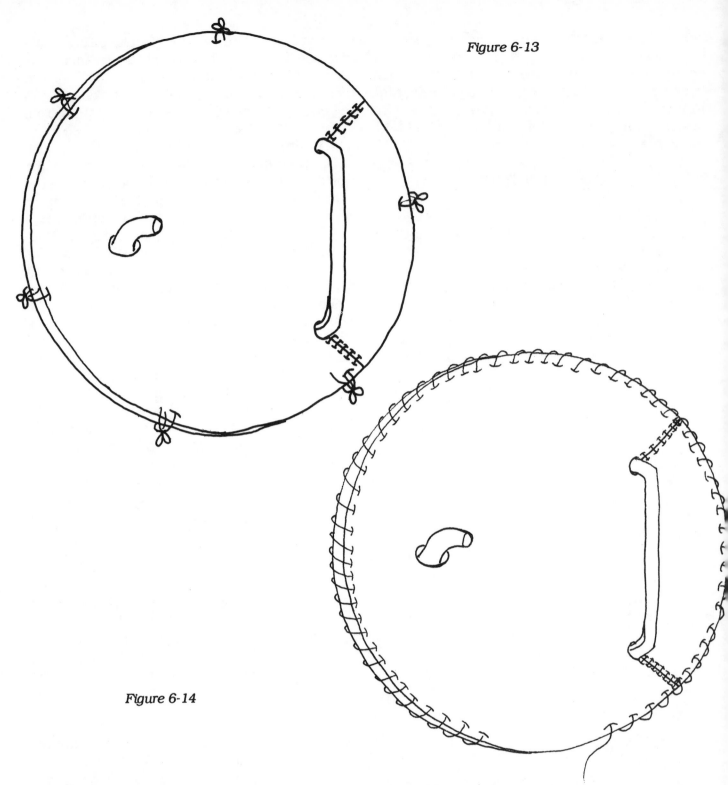

Figure 6-13

Figure 6-14

Stitch the two pieces of buckskin together around the buckle blank (Figure 6-14). Pull or cut the tacking stitches and remove them as the stitching approaches.

BEADED EDGING

Bead the border of the buckle with a Gourd Stitch using dark red and pink beads in equal parts. Start the first row at any point around the outside edge of the beadwork and alternate stitching eight red and then eight pink beads with a Two Bead Return Stitch close to the rest of the beadwork. Since the edging is worked in a circle, use a regular Gourd Stitch rather than the Gourd Stitch Edging variation. Add subsequent rows in the network style of the Gourd Stitch (see Beading Techniques), alternating four red beads with four

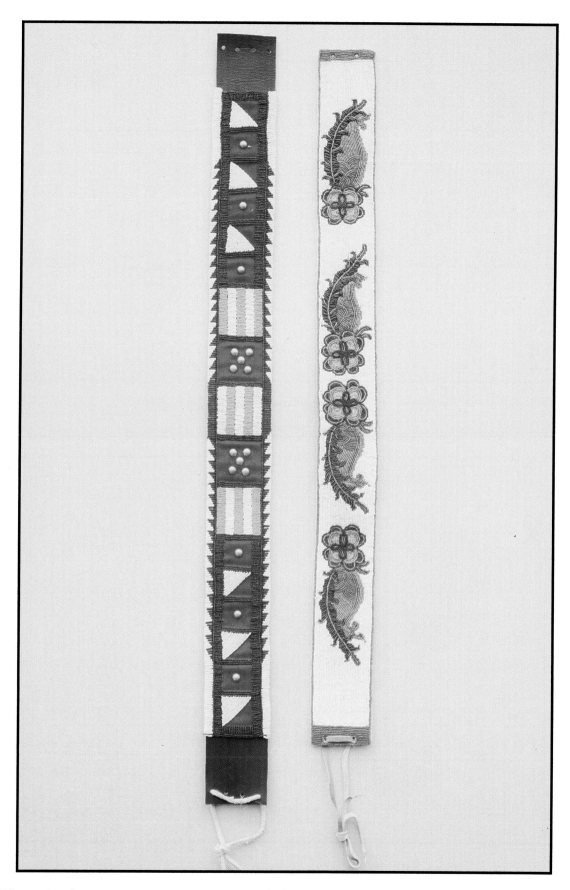

Plate I: Geometric Pattern Belt, left (pp 84-92) and Floral Belt (pp 93-103)

Plate II: Rosette Hair Ties (pp 21-26)

Plate III: Round Floral Belt Buckle (pp 43-53)

Plate IV: Neck Knife Sheath, top right (pp 54-62); Large Old Style Knife Sheath, bottom right (pp 63-72); and Wrap Around Knife Sheath, left (pp 73-83)

Plate V: Large Barrette, right (pp 9-13) and Heart Shaped Barrette, left (pp14-20)

pink beads. Figure 6-15 shows how this bead placement evolves into a spiral pattern. Notice how the second row pulls the beads not caught by a return stitch in the first row out of line, so that two rows appear as three. The photograph below also shows the spiral pattern that will automatically work into the edging. Add enough rows to the edging to wrap the beadwork around the edge of the buckle and cover the seam on the back. Stitch each bead in the last row to the leather on the back of the buckle.

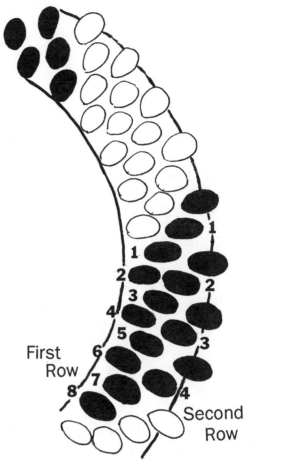

Figure 6-15

53

NECK KNIFE SHEATH

Materials

2	Buckskin Pieces - 3 1/2 " x 7"
1	Buckskin Piece - 5" x 7"
2	Rawhide or Medium Cowhide Pieces - 3" x 5 1/2"
1	Buckskin Thong - 32" long
1	Bobbin Nymo Beading Thread - Size A
1	Spool Cotton Thread - Size 16
4	Hanks Size 12/° Seed Beads:
	1 White, 1 Transparent Dark Blue,
	1 Mustard Yellow & 1 Light Blue

This sheath will fit most average sized patch knives or small skinning knives. It is fitted with a cord for wearing around the neck but it can also be tied on a belt. The beading pattern is heavily influenced by Sioux design.

LAYOUT

The patterns for this piece are provided in Figures 7-1 to 7-3 on grids where one square is equal to one square inch. Cut two sheath blanks from the pieces of rawhide or medium weight cowhide; two sheath covers from the 3 1/2 by 7 inch pieces of buckskin; and one fringe piece from the 5 by 7 inch piece of buckskin.

Select one of the cover pieces for the beading on the front of the sheath. Put masking tape on the back of this cover.

Draw the beading guidelines on the front of this cover piece. Begin by positioning one of the blank pieces about 1/4 inch from the bottom of the cover piece and centering it from side to side (Figure 7-4). Trace around the edge of the blank with a marking pen.

Remove the blank and draw a second line, 1/8 inch inside the first, along the sides and bottom of the outline (Figure 7-5). This second line marks the outside edge of the main design. The beadwork runs all the way to the top of the blank outline, so it is not necessary to draw a second line along the top edge.

Continue the layout by marking the center of the top line (point A in Figure 7-5). Measure 3/4 inch down from this top line and draw a line across the sheath. Find the center of this new line and mark it (B). Further divide this line into quarters with two small marks (C and D). The top left corner of the beadwork area is point E and the top right corner is point F.

Draw in the top triangular patterns by connecting points E and C, C and A, A and D, and finally D and F (see Figure 7-5).

Begin the lower set of triangles by drawing two new lines; draw the first 1/8 inch below line C-B-D, and the second 1 inch below line C-B-D. Find the center of the first new line and place a mark there (H). Do the same on the second new line (point K).

Still following Figure 7-5, divide the line marked H into quarters with small marks designated G and I. The left edge of line K is point J and the right edge point L. Draw in the second set of triangles by connecting points J and G, G and K, K and I, and finally I and L. The geometric design

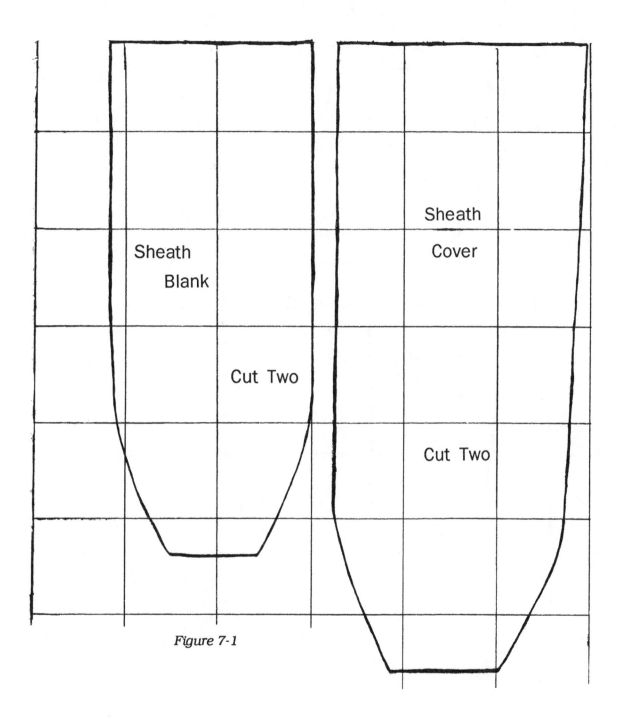

Sheath
Blank

Cut Two

Figure 7-1

Sheath
Cover

Cut Two

Figure 7-2

Figure 7-3

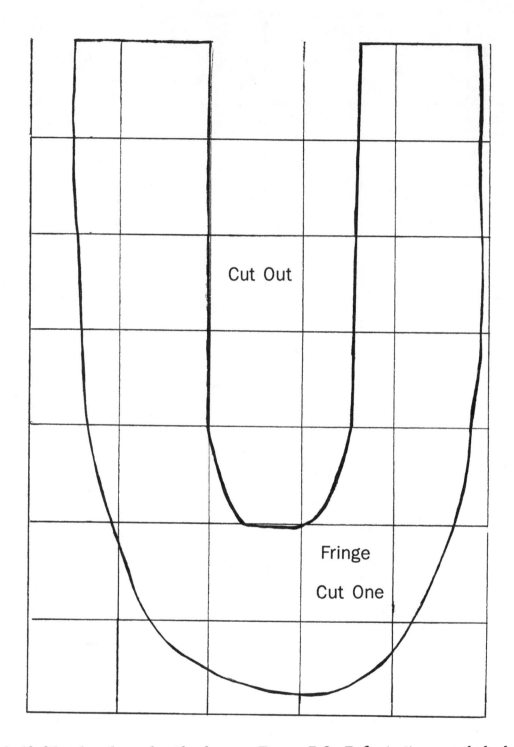

Cut Out

Fringe

Cut One

in the bottom half of the sheath need not be drawn as it is beaded with a bead by bead graph given later.

BEADING INSTRUCTIONS

A diagram of the knife sheath, color-keyed except for the geometric design, is provided in Figure 7-6. Refer to it as needed while beading.

Use a Three Bead Return Stitch and transparent dark blue beads to outline all but the top edge of the beadwork area. Start in the top right corner and bead on the 1/8 inch interior guideline around to the top left corner. Add a second row of dark blue to the outside of the first one. Finally, bead across the top line of the beadwork area with a single row of transparent dark blue beads (see Figure 7-6).

Continue to bead back and forth across the piece with a Three Bead Return Stitch. Add a row of white beads beneath the top outline and begin the top triangles in the third row. Figure 7-7 shows a detail of the bead arrangement for these two triangles. Each triangle has four mustard yellow beads on either edge, with an inner core of dark blue. The background is light blue. Follow the guidelines closely to maintain sharp edges on the triangles.

As the work progresses down the triangles, increase the number of light blue background beads on the sides and in the center of each row. At the same time, decrease the number of dark blue beads in the centers of the triangles; the number of mustard yellow beads remains the same (see Figure 7-7).

By the 8th row of this section, there will be no dark blue beads in the triangles. After this row, decrease the number of mustard yellow

Figure 7-4   Figure 7-5

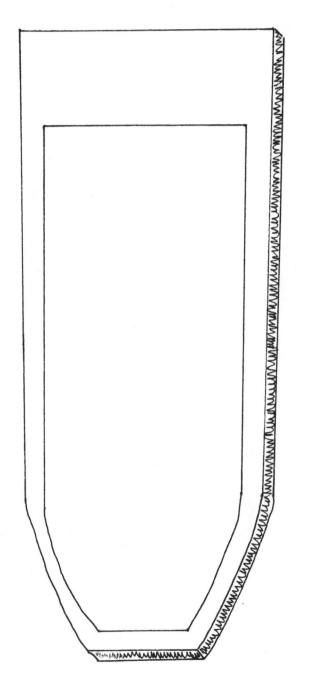
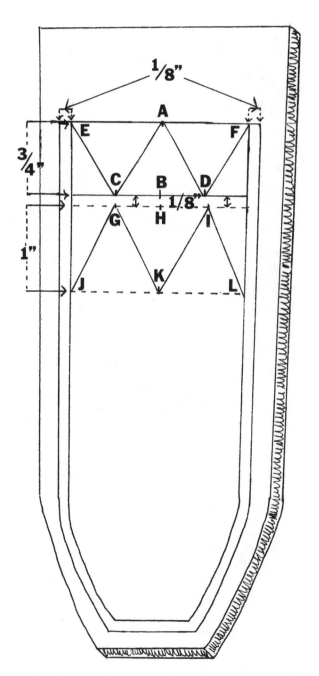

Figure 7-6

Figure 7-7

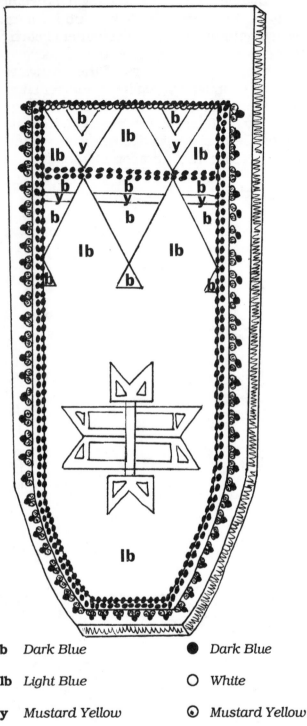

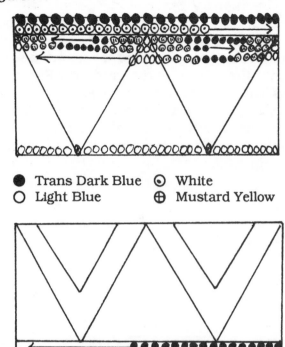

● Trans Dark Blue ☉ White
○ Light Blue ⊕ Mustard Yellow

Figure 7-8

b *Dark Blue* ● *Dark Blue*

lb *Light Blue* ○ *White*

y *Mustard Yellow* ☉ *Mustard Yellow*

beads inside the triangles. The final row in the top section will be light blue except for single mustard yellow beads at the point of each triangle.

Continue beading downward and start the next design section with two rows of dark blue beads (Figure 7-8).

The next set of triangular shapes begins in the third row of this section. Place a light blue

bead between the bases of each of the three dark blue triangles. Increase the number of light blue beads between triangles by two in each row (i.e. one in the third row, three in the second row, five in the third row, etc.). Decrease the number of beads inside the triangles proportionately. It may be necessary to crowd in an extra bead or stretch fewer beads across some areas in the design, as the beads must be made to fit within the guidelines and bead widths can vary. Be very careful if this seems to be the case and try above all else to follow the lines of the pattern as they are drawn on the leather.

Bead the 5th and 6th rows of this section with mustard yellow beads inside the triangles instead of dark blue; the background remains light blue. Use dark blue beads inside the triangles for the remainder of this section. Bead the last row with light blue beads except for single dark blue beads at the tip of each triangle.

The next row starts the small end triangles, which are located at the tips of the three triangles just finished (see Figure 7-8). Bead them with dark blue beads by making simple geometric bead increases in the next three rows. The background remains light blue. The graph in Figure 7-9 shows the number and placement of

Figure 7-9

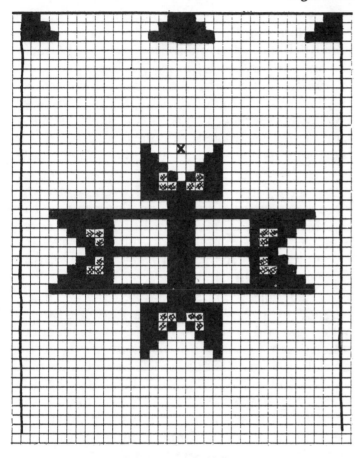

☐ *Light Blue*
■ *Transparent Dark Blue*
▨ *Mustard Yellow*

these beads. Each square in the graph represents a single bead and a legend is supplied for color reference.

When the small triangles are completed, add eleven rows of light blue beads. Then find the center of the next row, marked X in Figure 7-9. Use the graph as a reference for number and color of beads, and work from the center out to first one, and then the other edge of the beading area. This technique ensures that the geometric design will be properly centered.

Follow the bead pattern in Figure 7-9 and

bead the lower geometric design in the next 22 rows. It is not necessary to bead the rest of this pattern from the center out, but try to keep the design centered and be sure to adjust for any drift that occurs.

Fill the rest of the beadwork area with rows of light blue beads. Be sure to keep the rows straight and parallel to the rows of dark blue beads running along the bottom of the sheath. When the beadwork is finished, remove the tape from the back of the buckskin.

CONSTRUCTION

The sheath is now ready to be sewn together. Begin by punching a series of holes along the sides and bottom of one of the rawhide blank pieces. Start in the top right corner and punch the holes 1/16 inch from the edge with the

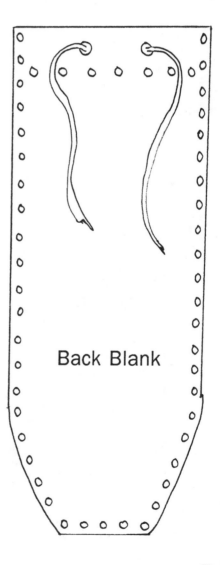

Back Blank

Figure 7-10

smallest awl available on the leather punch. Space the holes 1/4 inch apart and run them around the edge of the sheath to the top left corner (Figure 7-10).

Punch a matching series of holes in the second rawhide blank. The holes in the two pieces of rawhide must line up exactly. To do this, place the punched piece of rawhide on top of the unpunched one (like sides together so that the holes will match up when the pieces are stitched together). Mark through each hole with a pen and punch a matching set of holes in the second piece of rawhide using the marks as a guide.

Now run a row of holes across the top of each blank, about 1/2 inch down from the top edge. Again, be sure the holes in the two blanks

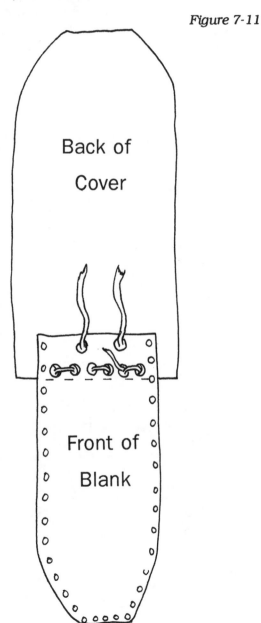

Figure 7-11

line up exactly. Select one of the blank pieces as the back of the sheath and punch two additional holes in it, centered above the top row (see Figure 7-10). These holes are for the neck thong and should be slightly larger than the rest of the holes. Thread the ends of the buckskin thong through these holes so that the ends come out on the grain side of the blank. Pull them through and center the thong between the holes.

The next step is to sew the two sheath covers to their respective blanks along the top edge. Note that the back sheath cover is the one which is not beaded and the back sheath blank is the one with the neck thong. The top of the cover is sewn to the top of the blank upside down so that the cover can be folded over the top of the blank. Lay both back pieces on a flat surface. The back side of the cover piece should face up and the back side of the blank piece should face down. Rotate the cover piece so that it is upside down and put the top edge of the blank over the straight edge of the cover. Position the blank so that the top row of holes is just above the edge of the cover and center it from side to side (Figure 7-11).

With the blank and cover pieces in this position, stitch them together through the punched holes, using a doubled heavy cotton thread, a Glover's needle and a Running Stitch. When the end of the row of stitching is reached, stitch back through the holes in the opposite direction, filling the spaces left between the previous stitches (see Figure 7-11). Sewing the pieces together in this manner and folding the cover over the top edge of the blank protects the neck thong from the knife sliding in and out, hides the blank and strengthens the top of the bag.

Sew the front cover and blank pieces together in the same manner. Center the top row of beading on the blank and position the cover so that this row will be even with the top edge of the sheath when the cover is folded over the blank.

Now sew the front and back of the sheath together. Put the cover/blank pieces together, with the fronts of the cover pieces facing each other. Place the fringe piece between the two blanks, so that it forms a welt in the seam between them (Figure 7-12). Stitch the blank front, blank back and fringe piece together through the holes around the edges of the blanks. Use a Running Stitch, heavy cotton thread and a Glover's needle. After sewing around the edge once, reverse direction and stitch around a second time, filling in the spaces left between the previous stitches.

Fold the back cover piece down over the back blank and mark the locations of the two neck thong holes. Raise the cover piece and punch two holes on the marks which match the two holes in the blank. Pass the neck thong through these holes.

Fold both cover pieces down over their respective blanks. Using the beading thread and needle, stitch the cover pieces together with a Running Stitch. Take very small stitches and pass the thread through both cover pieces and the fringe piece, just outside the edge of the sheath blanks (Figure 7-13). Trim the leather of

Figure 7-12

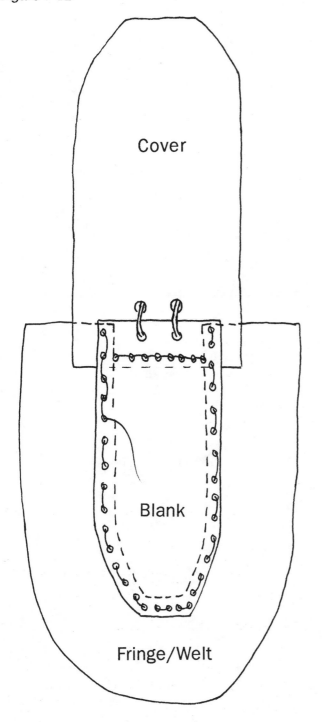

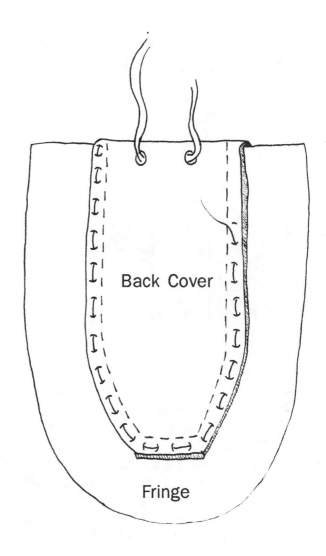

Figure 7-13

the cover pieces close to the stitching. Be careful not to cut any threads and do not trim the fringe piece.

If a belt sheath is preferred to a knife sheath, cut the ends of the thong to the right length for a belt loop and knot the ends together with a square knot.

Bead the edge of the sheath with a three bead Oblique Edging Stitch (Figure 7-14). Run the beaded edging next to the outside row of dark blue beads along the sides and bottom of the sheath (see Figure 7-6). The Two Bead Return base is mustard yellow and the top bead in each

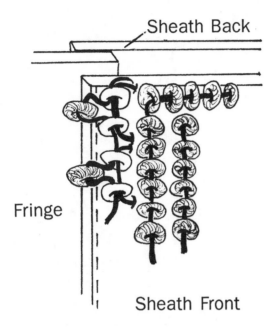

Sheath Back

Fringe

Sheath Front

Figure 7-14

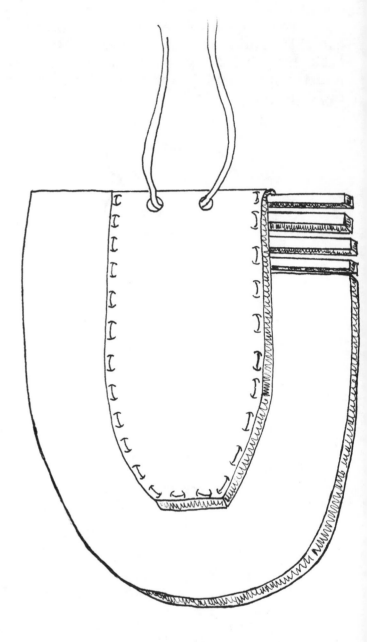

stitch is dark blue.

Complete the sheath by cutting the fringe piece into individual fringes not more than 1/8 inch wide (Figure 7-15). Be careful not to cut any threads. Narrow fringes are necessary on a small piece of beadwork such as this one; extremely wide fringing is overpowering and draws the eye away from the beadwork instead of framing it.

LARGE, OLD STYLE KNIFE SHEATH

Materials

3	Buckskin Pieces - 4 1/2" x 11"
1	Heavy Buckskin Piece - 1 3/4" x 7 1/2"
2	Rawhide or Medium Cowhide Pieces-3 1/2" x 9 1/2"
1	Small Spool Silk Beading Thread - Size A
1	Spool Cotton Thread - Size 16
3	Hanks Size 12/° Seed Beads:
	1 White, 1 Pony Trader Blue &
	1 Greasy Yellow

This Northern Plains style knife sheath will fit either a dagger or butcher type knife with a blade length of 6 inches. Though the colors and pattern were fairly common throughout the Plains area, checkerboard designs are most often associated with the Blackfoot Confederation. This sheath is worn on a belt.

LAYOUT

The patterns for this sheath are drawn to scale on grids in Figures 8-1 to 8-3. One square in the grids is equal to one square inch. Construct full size pattern pieces from heavy paper or Mylar as described in the Materials section at the beginning of the book. Cut two sheath blanks from the rawhide or cowhide and two sheath covers and one sheath welt from the three 4 1/2 by 11 inch pieces of buckskin.

Select one of the cover pieces for the front of the sheath and put strips of masking tape on the back or flesh side.

Draw the beading guidelines on the front of this cover piece. Begin by positioning one of the blank pieces on top of the cover piece about 1/2 inch from the bottom edge and centered from side to side. Trace around the blank with a marking pen (Figure 8-4).

Remove the blank and draw a second line 3/16 inch inside the first one, along the sides and bottom of the blank outline (see Figure 8-4). This second line marks the outside edge of the main design. The beadwork runs all the way to the top of the blank outline, so there is no need to draw a second line along the top edge.

Continue the beading pattern layout with the top section. Draw five horizontal lines across the top of the beadwork area, beginning 3/8 inch below the top edge and spacing the lines 3/8 inch apart (Figure 8-5). This divides the top section into five horizontal beading rows.

Move to the bottom section, which begins directly below the lines just drawn. Make a series of marks across the top of this section which are 3/8 inch apart. Make a similar series of marks across the bottom of the section which are 5/16 inch apart. The marks along the bottom are closer together than the ones on the top to compensate for the taper in the sheath. The rows of beadwork will also have to taper slightly from top to bottom. Connect the corresponding marks with vertical lines, dividing the bottom section into seven vertical beading rows (see Figure 8-5).

The small squares of the mountain design in the top section are all 5/16 inch wide (Figure 8-6). Begin to layout this design by finding the center of the top line (point A) and the center of the 5th line (point B). Make a small mark at each

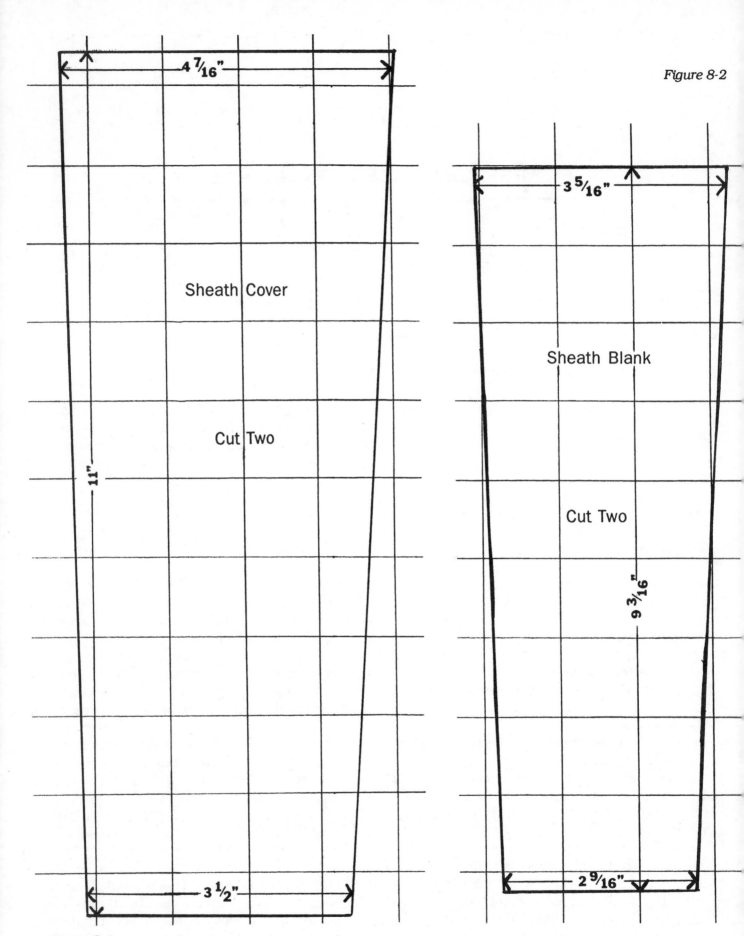

Figure 8-2

4 7/16"

Sheath Cover

Cut Two

11"

3 1/2"

Figure 8-1

3 5/16"

Sheath Blank

Cut Two

9 3/16"

2 9/16"

64

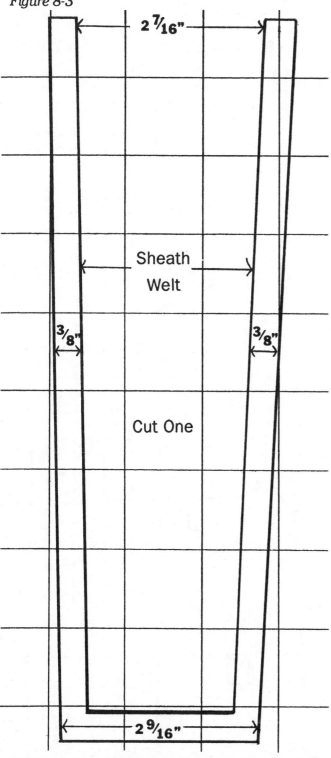

Figure 8-3

2 $\frac{7}{16}$"

Sheath
Welt

$\frac{3}{8}$" $\frac{3}{8}$"

Cut One

2 $\frac{9}{16}$"

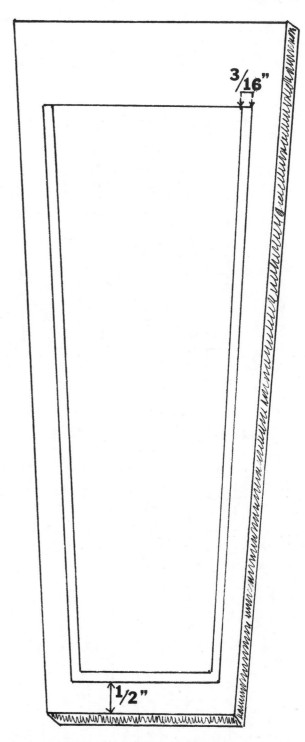

Figure 8-4

$\frac{3}{16}$"

$\frac{1}{2}$"

point. Then make small marks 5/32 inch to either side of each of these points. Connect these new marks with two vertical lines extending from the first to the 5th horizontal lines. This creates the first set of squares.

Following Figure 8-6, make the next set of squares by drawing two more vertical lines, 5/16 inch to either side of the lines just drawn, which

extend from line 2 to line 6. Mark the 5/16 points on lines two and five before drawing these new vertical lines. The rest of the vertical lines are also spaced 5/16 inch apart; the third set extends from line 3 to line 6, the fourth set from line 4 to line 6, and the final set from line 5 to line 6. This last set of lines marks the location of a single line of white beads on either end of the bottom hori-

Figure 8-5

Figure 8-6 (upside down)

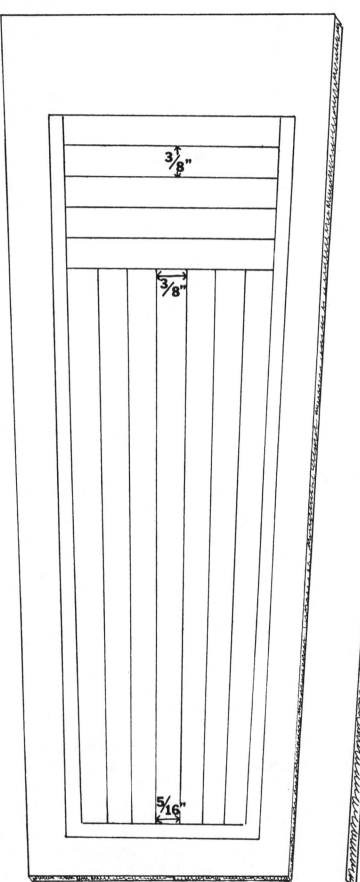

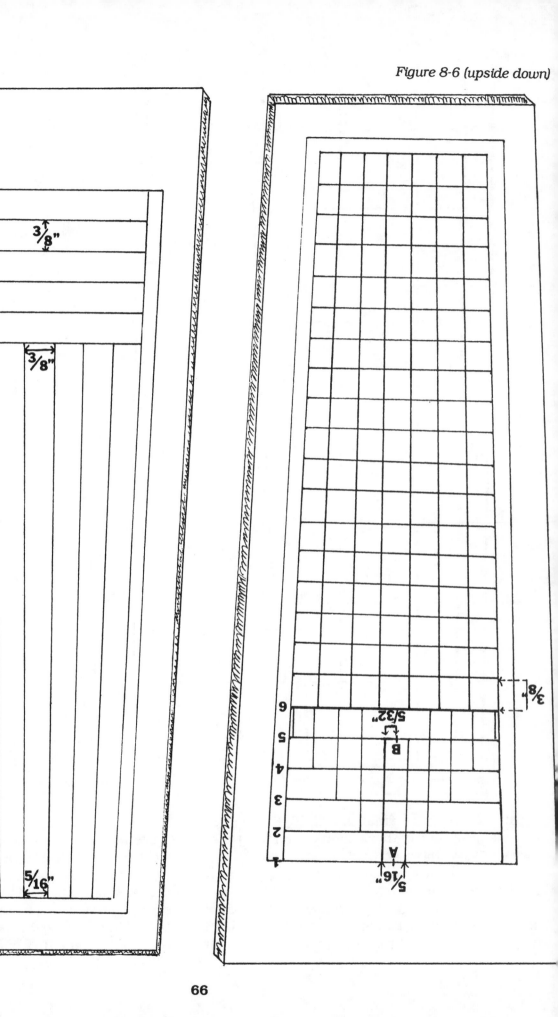

zontal row.

Figure 8-6 also shows the bottom section laid out into squares. These are formed by drawing 17 horizontal lines, 3/8 inch apart, across the seven vertical lines already drawn. To keep these lines straight, place sets of small marks on both sides of the sheath, each 3/8 inch below the preceding line and then connect the marks with a new line.

It is possible to begin beading at this point, however it is highly advisable to mark each of the colored squares first. A color-keyed diagram is provided in Figure 8-7. Following this, place a b in each of the blue squares and a y in each of the yellow squares on the sheath cover. Leave the white squares blank. This will make the beadwork less confusing, enabling each row to be done at a much faster pace.

BEADING INSTRUCTIONS

Begin beading in the top right corner of the beadwork area with a Lazy Stitch (point C in Figure 8-8). Bead across the knife sheath, from right to left, with stitches that go back and forth between the top and bottom of the first horizontal row. It should take about eight beads to go across

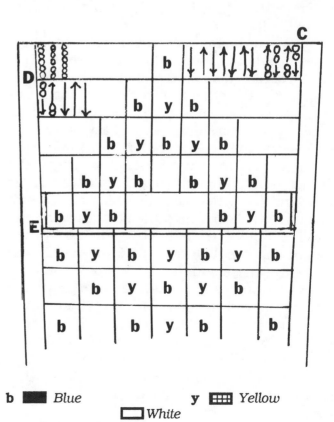

b ■ Blue   y ▦ Yellow
□ White

Figure 8-7   Figure 8-8

67

the row from top to bottom, but be sure to check this and add or subtract beads if necessary. Make sure the stitches are parallel to one another and pull each one tight before adding the beads for the next stitch. Be especially careful to check the number of beads needed as the colors change. There can be slight differences in bead size from color to color, making a small variation in the number of beads necessary.

When the first row is completed from right to left, work the second row from left to right, starting at point D in Figure 8-8. Align the stitches in the second row beneath the corresponding stitches in the first row, so that a straight line of beads is maintained down this section of the sheath. Some slight adjustments may be necessary to account for the decreasing width of the sheath.

The sheath may be turned upside down to work the second row so that the beadwork is actually done from right to left, as is natural for a right handed beader. Bead the other three horizontal rows in the top section, following the color changes in Figures 8-7 and 8-8. Work back and forth across the sheath from row to row. The rows are worked in this fashion so that the thread does not have to be knotted at the end of each row. Do not forget the single line of white beads on either end of the last row.

When the top section is completed, begin to bead the bottom section in vertical rows. This change of direction visually divides the two sections from each other and is a good design concept to remember - it is quite often used in larger pieces of beadwork done with a Lazy Stitch.

Start the bottom section in the upper left corner (point E in Figure 8-8) and bead down the sheath from top to bottom with stitches that go back and forth between the sides of the first vertical row. Again, keep the stitches snug and parallel. Note that the top two stitches in each row are white (see Figures 8-7 & 8-8), even though the rest of these squares are colored. Bead all seven vertical rows, working up and down the sheath to move from row to row. Align the stitches in each row with the stitches in the previous row, horizontally this time, so that a straight line of beads is maintained across the sheath.

When the main design (inside the border) is finished, remove the tape from the back of the work.

Figure 8-9

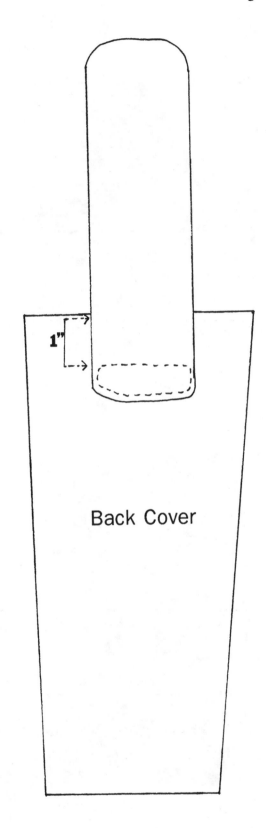

Back Cover

1"

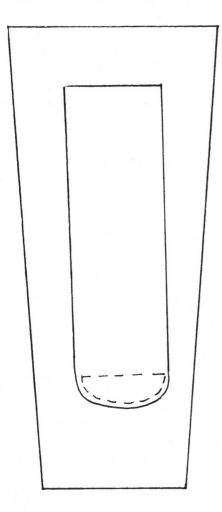

Figure 8-10

CONSTRUCTION

The first construction step is the addition of the belt loop to the back cover of the sheath. The strip of heavy buckskin is the belt loop piece. Round the corners of this strip with a pair of scissors. The top of the belt loop is sewn upside down to the top of the back cover piece, so that the loop can be folded down over the stitching. To do this, place the belt loop upside down on the back cover piece as shown in Figure 8-9. Position it so that the top of the stitching will be 1 inch from the top of the cover piece. The grain side of the cover piece should face up and the flesh side of the belt loop should face up. This places the two grain sides together, face to face, so that the smooth or grain side of the loop leather will face out when it is folded down over the stitching.

Stitch an elongated semi-circle near the end of the belt loop with a Running Stitch, heavy cotton thread and a Glover's needle. Keep the stitching as small and tight as possible. After stitching around the strip once, reverse direction and stitch back around the semi-circle, filling in the gaps between stitches. Fold the buckskin strip down onto the back cover, as shown in Figure 8-10. Stitch the bottom of the loop to the the cover in the same manner as the top. This bottom stitching will remain exposed.

Next, punch a series of holes in one of the rawhide blanks (Figure 8-11). Use the smallest awl in the leather punch and start in either top corner. Punch the holes 1/16 inch from the edge, about 1/2 inch apart, along the sides and bottom. Place this piece over the second blank piece, like sides together, and mark the positions of the holes on the second blank with a pen or pencil. Punch a matching set of holes in the second blank, using the marks as a guide. Finally punch a row of holes 1/2 inch down from the top edge of each blank. These holes should be 1/4 inch apart.

Next, sew the two sheath covers to their respective blanks along the top edges. Similar to the belt loop, sew the top edge of each cover upside down to the top of the blank, but behind it so that the cover can be folded over the top of the blank. Sew the back pieces first. Place the back cover piece upside down on the work surface, with the flesh side facing up. Put one of the blank pieces on top of it, so that the top row of holes is just above the edge of the cover piece (Figure 8-

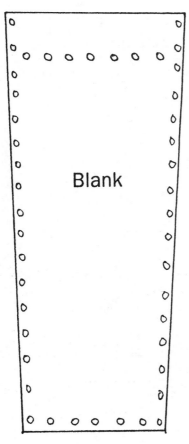

Blank

Figure 8-11

69

12). Stitch the two pieces together through the top row of holes with heavy cotton thread, a Glover's needle and a Running Stitch. When the end of the row is reached, reverse direction and stitch back through the holes again, filling in the gaps between the previous stitches.

Stitch the front cover to the second blank piece in the same manner, making sure that the beadwork is centered on the blank and that the top row of beading will be even with the top edge of the sheath when the cover is folded over the blank.

Figure 8-12

Figure 8-13

Figure 8-14

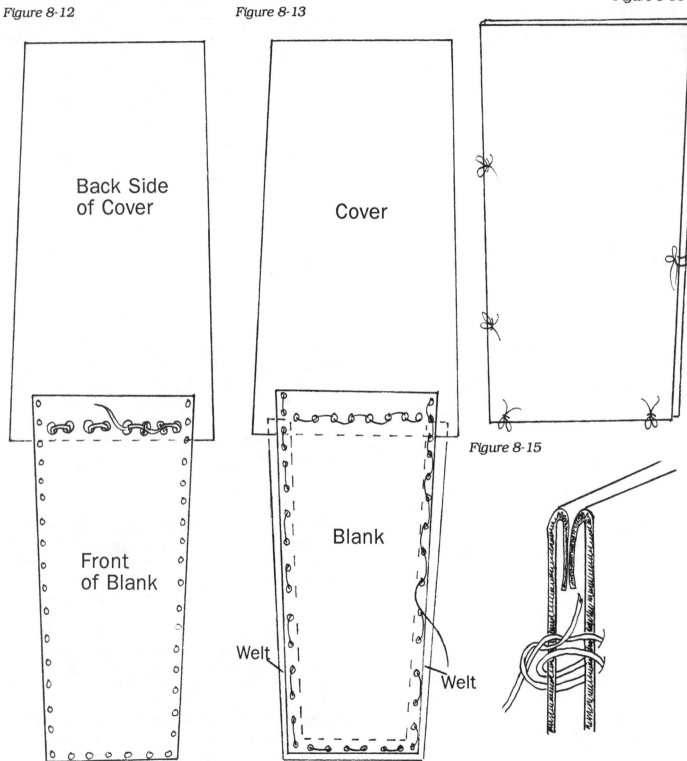

Figure 8-15

70

When this is done, sew the front and back of the sheath together. Put the cover/blank pieces together with the fronts of the cover pieces facing one another. Trim the top 1/4 inch off both sides of the welt piece and insert it between the two blank pieces. The welt should sit between the edges of the blanks, from the top row of holes down (Figure 8-13).

Still using a Glover's needle, heavy cotton thread and a Running Stitch, start in one of the upper corners of the blanks and sew the blanks together with the welt in the seam. Stitch through the holes punched around the sides and bottom. When one row of stitching is completed around the edge of the blanks, reverse direction and stitch back around the sheath, filling in the gaps between the previous stitches (see Figure 8-13).

Fold the two cover pieces down over the sheath blanks. Prepare to sew the cover pieces around the blanks by tacking them together with a beading needle and thread in five places as shown in Figure 8-14. Put two tacks on the bottom, two on the left side and one halfway down the right side. A detail of how these tacks are

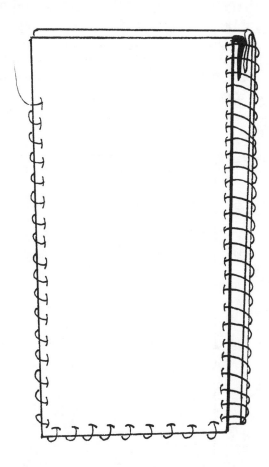

Figure 8-16

Figure 8-17

☐   *White*

▦   *Greasy Yellow*

■   *Pony Trader Blue*

71

made is given in Figure 8-15; basically they are two Whip Stitches tied off with a square knot. If the cover pieces seem a bit too large, trim off the excess buckskin so that the edges just overlap. Be sure to tighten the covers evenly around the blanks and keep the beadwork centered on the front as the tacks are made.

Start in the upper right corner of the sheath (the place farthest from any tacking) and stitch the cover pieces together with a Whip Stitch and the beading thread and needle (Figure 8-16).

BEADED EDGING

Cover the outside edges and stitching of the sheath with a Lazy Stitch seam cover. The color-keyed diagram in Figure 8-17 shows how the edge beading becomes a part of the main design. Use this Figure as a guide and place marks along the sides and bottom of the sheath to indicate color changes in the edge beading. Mark a square of blue on either side of the 2nd, 9th, 10th and 17th rows in the bottom section. Divide the bottom edge into squares which match the main design. Mark the bottom corners blue and alternate squares of yellow and blue in between.

Begin the edge beading at the top of the sheath, on either side, next to the main beadwork area. Bead towards the bottom, making sure

Figure 8-18

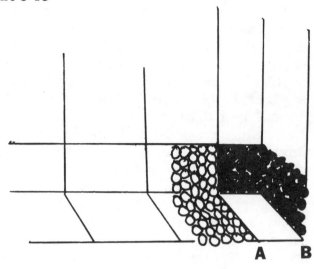

● Pony Trader Blue   ○ Greasy Yellow

there are enough beads in each stitch to completely cover the seam on both sides of the sheath. Stop when the bottom is reached and bead down the other side. Next, start at one edge of the main beadwork area and bead across the bottom of the sheath to the other edge of the main design. This leaves the bottom edges of the two corners of the sheath unbeaded (Figure 8-18). Fill these squares with horizontal rows of blue beads running from the bottom edging at point A to the final row of beads in the side edging at point B.

WRAP AROUND KNIFE SHEATH

Materials
1   Thick White Rawhide Piece - 8" x 11"
1   Heavy Cowhide Piece - 7" x 3"
1   Red Wool Piece - 13" x 6"
1   Thick White Buckskin Thong - 15" long
1   Spool Cotton Sewing Thread - Size 16
1   Bobbin Nylon Beading Thread - Size A
4   Hanks Size 12/° Seed Beads:
1 Transparent Dark Blue, 1 Mustard Yellow,
1 Rose White-Heart & 1 White
1   Sharps Sewing Needle (eye to match cotton thread)
1   Craft Knife with a narrow blade

The style, colors and materials of this knife sheath mark it as from an early era. It is constructed of a single piece of rawhide, which is folded or wrapped around the blade and stitched up one side. The beadwork, in a pattern common among many tribes, is done on red wool and the fabric color is incorporated into the design. The result is an attractive looking project with a minimum amount of time expended on the actual beadwork.

This sheath is worn by running the belt over the plain part of the rawhide and then through the slot on the left side. It fits a knife with a 6 inch blade.

PATTERNS

This sheath is constructed before the design pattern is laid out and beaded; the beading is then done on the wool with stitches that go into, but not through the material.

The patterns for this sheath are drawn to scale in Figures 9-1 to 9-3. The pattern pieces are on grids where one square equals one square inch. Construct full size pattern pieces from heavy paper or Mylar as described in the Materials section at the beginning of the book.

Trace the sheath pattern and cutout areas on the flesh side of the heavy white rawhide. Cut one sheath piece using heavy shears and then use a craft knife, such as an Exacto, to cut out the belt slot areas. Trace the welt pattern on the heavy cowhide and cut one welt piece with heavy leather shears. Trace the beading surface pattern on the wool and cut out one piece with a lighter pair of shears.

CONSTRUCTION

The first construction step is to punch holes in the rawhide and leather. Start with the sheath rawhide, grain side up. Mark a light pencil line, as shown in Figure 9-4, from the bottom of the left cutout (point A) to point B, which is 1 1/4 inches from the bottom edge, on the fold line. This line should follow the outside curve of the sheath and be 1 1/4 inches from the edge at all points. It is a guideline for the construction holes. Note that when the sheath piece is folded, the left side will become the front of the sheath and the right side will become the back. This can be reversed to make a sheath for a left handed person.

73

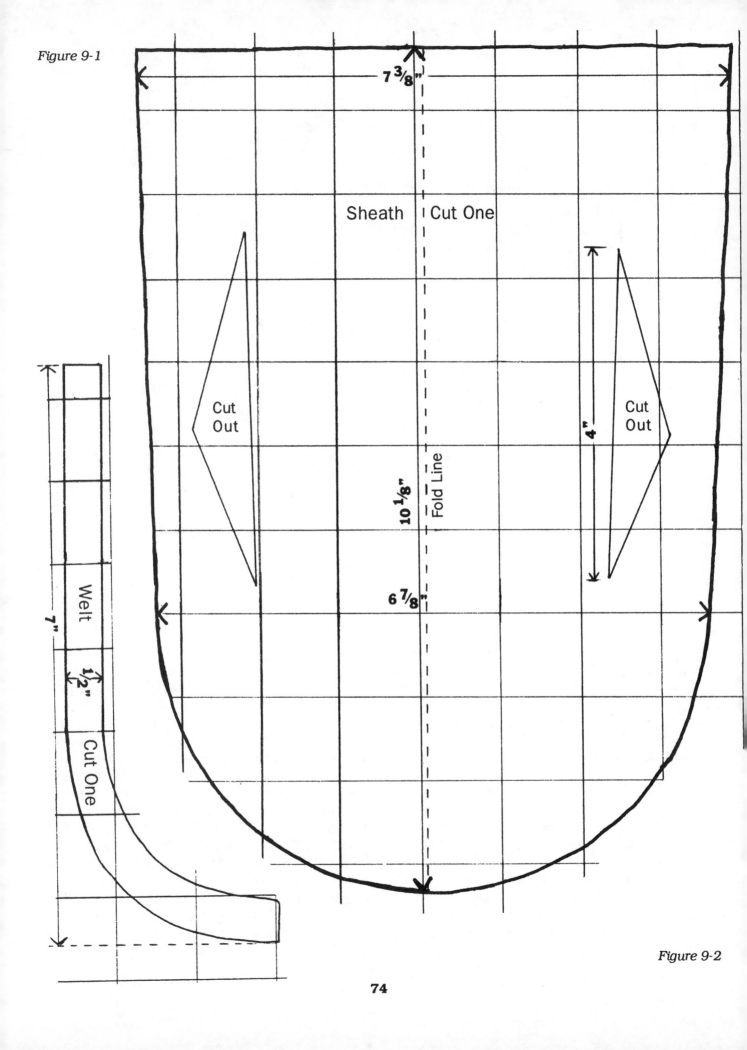

Figure 9-1

Sheath ¦ Cut One

7 3/8"

Cut
Out

Cut
Out

4"

10 1/8"

Fold Line

6 7/8"

Welt

7"

1/2"

Cut One

Figure 9-2

74

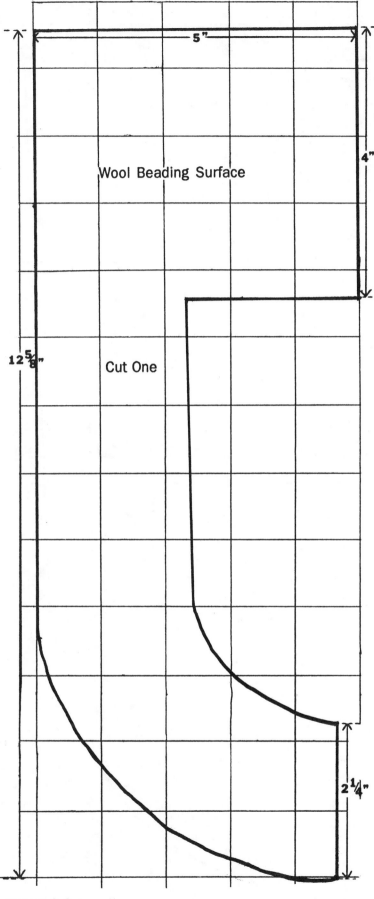

5"

Wool Beading Surface

4"

12⅝"

Cut One

2¼"

Figure 9-3

Select a medium sized awl on the leather punch and punch a series of holes, about 3/8 inch apart, inside the guideline just drawn. Start at point B and continue past point A along the inside of the left cutout to point C, which is just below the top of the belt cutout. The holes should be about 1/8 inch from the guideline and from the edge of the cutout (see Figure 9-4).

Use a sewing awl to punch a series of smaller holes, 1/4 inch apart, from point C straight across the sheath to point D on the fold line. Continue punching smaller holes up along the inside edge of the fold line to point E, which is 3/8 inch below the top edge of the sheath, then back across the sheath horizontally to point F, 3/16 inch from the left edge (see Figure 9-4).

Place the leather welt beneath the row of large holes and mark each hole on the welt with a pen. Punch holes on these marks with the same leather punch awl as was used to punch the large holes in the rawhide. This is the most accurate method of matching sewing holes for a perfect seam.

Fold the sheath piece along the fold line, so that the right or back half is under the left or front half. Again, use a pen to mark the location of each of the large holes on the back half of the sheath. Unfold the sheath piece and punch holes on each of the marks, using the same punch awl as before.

Next attach the red wool beading surface to the front half of the sheath. Place the wool piece on top of the front (left) half of the sheath rawhide, so that the curved inner edge of the wool follows the guideline drawn for the row of large holes (Figure 9-5). Fold the top edge of the wool over the top edge of the rawhide (line V-W in Figure 9-5). Draw a pencil guideline along the edge of the wool on the back of the rawhide, marking the location of the edge when the wool is folded. This guideline is used to keep the wool straight as it is sewn to the rawhide.

Set the two pieces on a flat surface, leaving the top edge of the wool in place over the top edge of the rawhide. Fold the

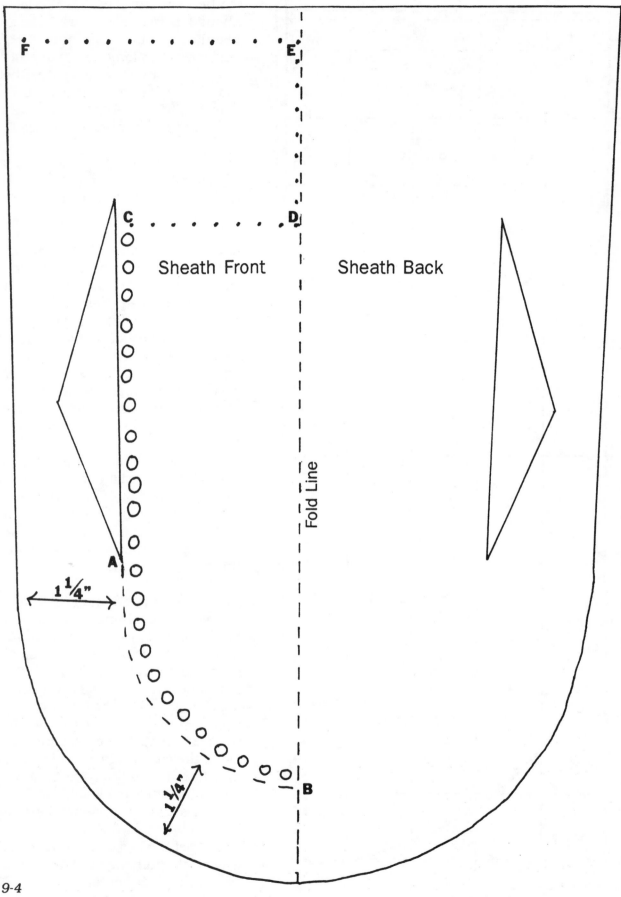

F • • • • • • • • • • E

C • • • • • • D

Sheath Front   Sheath Back

A

1¼"

Fold Line

1¼"

B

Figure 9-4

76

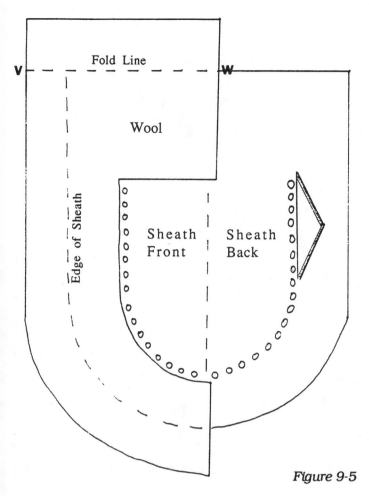

Figure 9-5

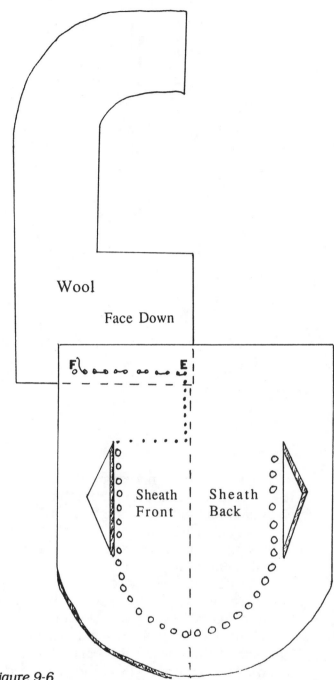

Figure 9-6

bottom of the wool piece up, so that the entire wool piece is upside down with the edge of the wool under the top edge of the rawhide piece (Figure 9-6). The beading side of the wool will face down, while the grain side of the rawhide remains up.

Hold the wool in this position and stitch it to the top edge of the rawhide with heavy cotton thread, a Sharps sewing needle and a Running Stitch. Start next to the fold line at point E and stitch towards point F, passing through the small holes previously punched. Make sure the wool stays lined up on the guideline drawn on the back of the rawhide. Leave the last hole in this row unstitched for now and end with the needle and thread on the grain or front side of the rawhide (see Figure 9-6).

Fold the wool back down over the rawhide so that the curved inner edge lines up along the row of large holes as before (Figure 9-7). At this point the needle and thread are between the wool and the rawhide. Carefully push the needle up through the wool as it lies in its proper position. Take a stitch through both wool layers and the

rawhide between them, using the empty hole at point F. This stitch helps lock the wool in position. Reverse direction and come back through the second hole in this line. Stitch the wool to the grain side of the rawhide, going across the top edge from point F to point E with a Running Stitch. Although only one row of stitching will show on the front of the sheath, this second row will fill the gaps between the previous stitches on the back of the sheath. Continue stitching down along the fold line to point D, then back across the sheath to point C, still using the small holes

77

Figure 9-8

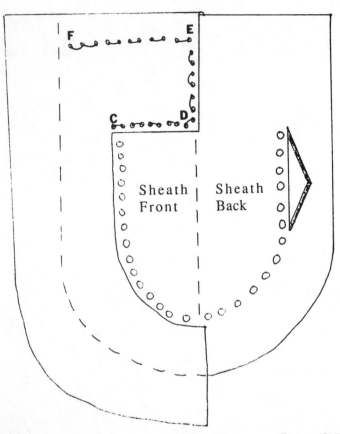

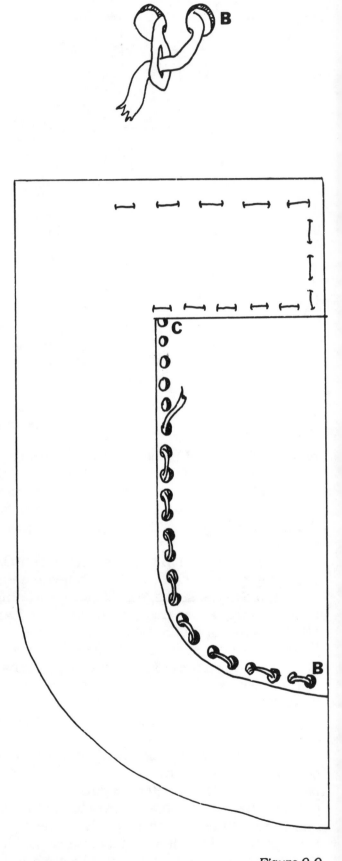

Figure 9-7

previously punched. If necessary, trim the edge of the wool so that it is 1/4 inch from the stitching which goes from point E to points D and C.

Sew the sheath together with the 15 inch leather thong. First fold the sheath on the center fold line as before. Insert the heavy leather welt between the two thicknesses of rawhide and align the three sets of large holes. Start at the bottom of the row of large holes, by the fold line. To knot the thong, thread it into the second hole and cut a small slit in the end on the back side of the sheath with a craft knife. Pass the other end of the thong through the first hole, then through the slit and on to the third hole (Figure 9-8). This is the easiest and most common method of knotting a thong to begin a row of stitching.

Stitch from the bottom (point B in Figure 9-9) to point C at the top of the row with a Running Stitch. Moisten and twist the end of the thong before pushing it through the holes. Pull the stitches as tight as possible. Knot the thong on the back of the sheath by tying two half hitches on the previous stitch. Follow the arrows and the numbered sequence in Figure 9-10 to tie this knot.

Figure 9-9

Lift the loose part of the wool off the rawhide and use a sewing awl to punch a series of holes around the remaining edges, through both thicknesses of rawhide (Figure 9-11). The holes should be no more than 1/4 inch apart and run from point W at the top left corner, down along the outside edge of the sheath to point X at the fold line; then up the fold line to point Y, just below the thong stitches; then up along the inner edge, just below the previous stitching and finally around the outside two edges of the belt cutout to point Z.

Lay the wool back down on the rawhide. Cut a slash from the edge of the wool at the center of the belt cutout (point A in Figure 9-12) to point B, which is about 1/4 inch from the opposite side of the cutout. The slash enables the wool to be folded around the rawhide without puckering.

Fold the wool around the left or outside edges of the rawhide belt cutout. If there is a pucker when the wool is folded, enlarge the slash a tiny bit so that the wool lays smoothly around the edge. Stitch the inner edge of the wool to the rawhide, going from point Z to point Y. Use heavy cotton thread, a Sharps sewing needle and a Running Stitch (Figure 9-13). Stitch through the small holes just punched in both thicknesses of rawhide and be sure to catch both thicknesses of wool around the cutout. Do not tie off the end of the thread.

Fold the wool around the sheath fold line and the outside edge of the rawhide. Continue stitching from point Y down to point X and then around the outside edge, up to point W. Again, be sure to catch both thicknesses of rawhide and

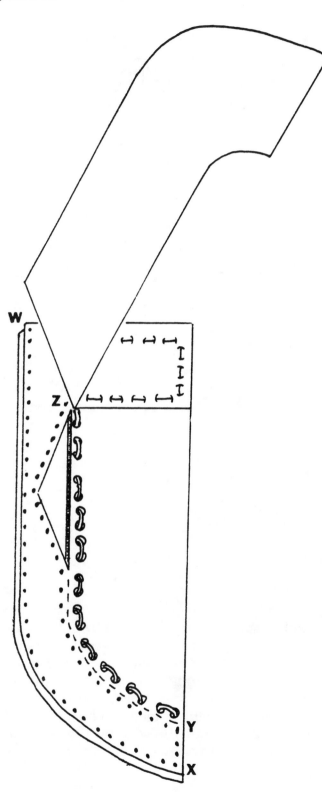

Figure 9-11

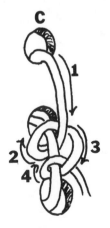

Figure 9-10

Figure 9-12

Figure 9-13

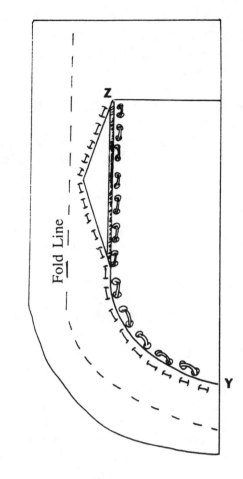

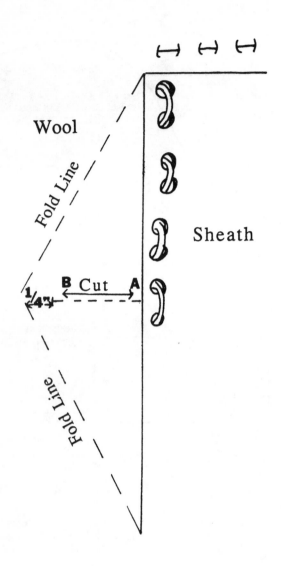

Wool

Fold Line

Sheath

B Cut A

1/4"

Fold Line

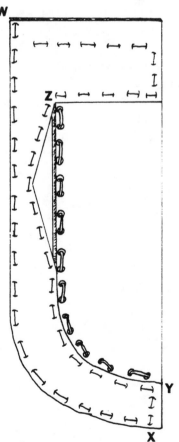

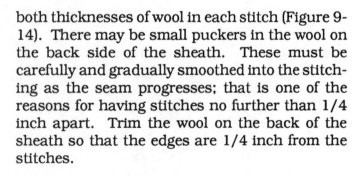

both thicknesses of wool in each stitch (Figure 9-14). There may be small puckers in the wool on the back side of the sheath. These must be carefully and gradually smoothed into the stitching as the seam progresses; that is one of the reasons for having stitches no further than 1/4 inch apart. Trim the wool on the back of the sheath so that the edges are 1/4 inch from the stitches.

LAYOUT

To simplify the layout instructions, place the sheath so that the fold line is on the right and

Figure 9-14

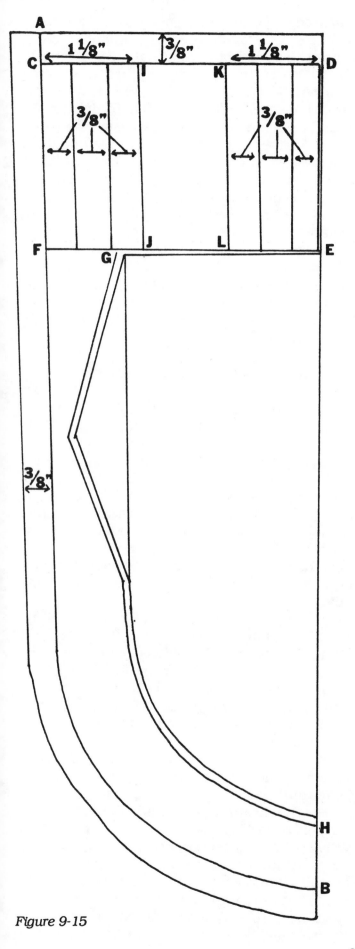

Figure 9-15

the belt cutout is on the left. The wool is divided into two sections: the top section is above the uncovered rawhide and the belt cutout; the bottom section is below the top section and goes around the left side and bottom of the uncovered rawhide.

Use a marking pen to draw the beading guidelines, defining the two main beading areas and the border areas first.

Follow Figure 9-15 and draw a border line, 3/8 inch from the left edge of the sheath. This line goes from point A (3/8 inch to the right of the top left corner) around the edge of the sheath to point B (3/8 inch above the bottom right corner).

Next, outline the top section of the wool. Draw a line 3/8 inch down from the top edge of the sheath, from line A-B (start at point C) to just outside the row of stitching on the fold line (point D). This line (C-D) separates the top border from the main beading area.

Draw a line along the right edge of this section, just outside the row of stitching. Go from point D, which is 3/8 inch below the top edge, to point E, just below the row of stitches at the bottom edge of the wool.

Draw another line along the bottom edge of this section, just below the row of stitches. Go from point E across the sheath, intersecting line A-B at point F.

Finish outlining the bottom beading area by drawing a line along the inner edge between the construction stitches and the edge of the wool. Start at the top of the belt cutout (point G) and go around the left edges of the cutout, then down around the curved edge of the wool to the

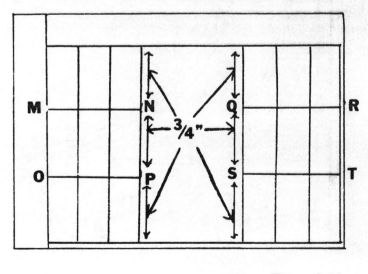

Figure 9-16

81

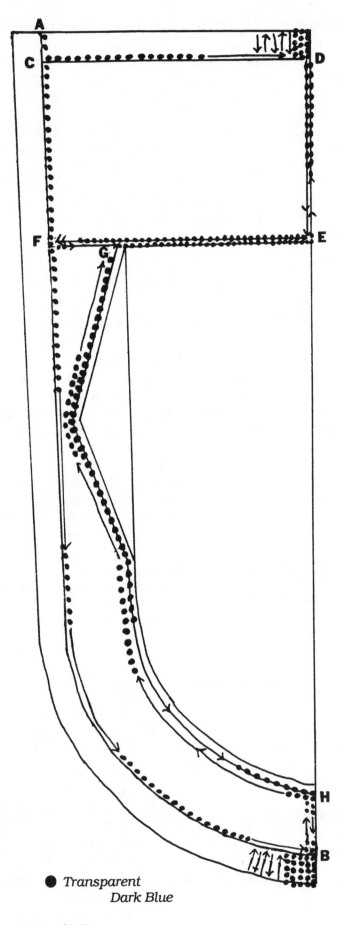

● Transparent
   Dark Blue

Figure 9-17

folded edge of the sheath (point H). This line must be close to the stitches so that a double row of beads will cover both the line and the stitches.

Divide the top beading area into thirds with vertical lines I-J and K-L (see Figure 9-15). These lines are 1 1/8 inches from the left (line E-F) and right (line C-D) borders, respectively.

Further divide the right and left sections just created into three vertical rows, each 3/8 inch wide. Leave the center section undivided.

Divide the right and left sections into thirds again, this time horizontally to create nine equal rectangles on each side (Figure 9-16). These horizontal lines (lines M-N/Q-R and O-P/S-T) are 3/4 inch from the top and bottom guidelines of the section and are 3/4 inch apart. Mark the end points of each of the lines before drawing them and make sure that they divide the space into equal thirds.

BEADING INSTRUCTIONS

Bead the border areas of this piece first. Begin on the top left at point A (Figure 9-17) and use a Three Bead Return Stitch. Run a row of transparent navy blue beads, just inside the left border guideline, down to point B at the bottom of the sheath. At point B, begin Lazy Stitching around the outside edge of the sheath. Go from the fold line back up to point A. Make sure that the beads go around the edge to the back of the sheath, but do not worry about covering the back stitching. This will take about eleven beads per stitch.

Again use a Three Bead Return Stitch and bead from point C across the top of the sheath to point D, then down the right edge to point E and back across the sheath to point F. From point C to point D the beads should be just above the guideline, however from point D to points E and F, the beads must run on top of the guideline (see Figure 9-17).

At point F, reverse the direction of the stitching and bead a second row of navy blue beads outside the row just completed. Bead back across the sheath to point E and then up to point D. This row will run very close to the edge of the wool and will almost obscure it (see Figure 9-17).

Bead another border of Lazy Stitch along the top of the sheath from point D to point C. The beads in this row should just reach the top of the sheath. This should also take about eleven beads per stitch.

The last double row of border work lies along the belt cutout and the inner edge of the wool from point G to point H, then down to point B. Use transparent navy blue beads and a Three Bead Return Stitch. Bead the first row on top of the guideline, then down the fold line. Reverse direction at point B and add a second row of beads, inside the first. Be sure to cover the construction stitching from point H to point G (see Figure 9-17).

Start the design work in the top section by

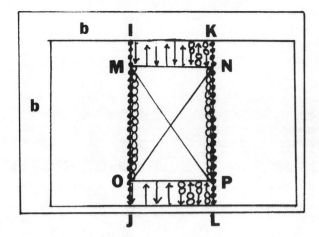

●   *Transparent Dark Blue*
○   *White*
b   *Transparent Dark Blue Border*

Figure 9-19

line from point M to point P across the middle of the area. Draw another line from point N to point O. Bead these lines with white beads and a Two Bead Return Stitch. Be sure that the beads hide the guidelines, as no other beading is done in this middle area.

The left side of the top section is beaded next, followed by the right side. Both sides have the same color pattern. In Figure 9-20, this color pattern is marked on the right side and the placement of the first row is shown on the left side. Bead each of these areas with three vertical rows of Lazy Stitch, stitching down the first row, then up the second and down the third. Alternate the colors of the rectangles, switching bead colors at each horizontal guideline and between each of the vertical rows.

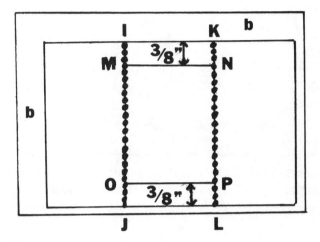

●   *Transparent Dark Blue*
b   *Transparent Dark Blue Border*

Figure 9-18

beading a row of transparent navy blue beads on top of lines I-J and K-L (Figure 9-18) with a Three Bead Return Stitch. Each of the three design areas in the top section is now outlined with navy blue beads.

Draw a line 3/8 inch from the top of the middle design area and another 3/8 inch from the bottom of this area (lines M-N and O-P in Figure 9-18). Lazy Stitch across the top and bottom of this section with white beads. Bead from just inside the navy blue outline at I-M across to K-N and from O-J across to P-L (Figure 9-19).

Begin at point M and use a Two Bead Return Stitch to bead a line of white beads, just inside the navy blue outline, down to point O. Bead a similar line from point N down to point P (see Figure 9-19).

Use a marking pen and a ruler to draw a

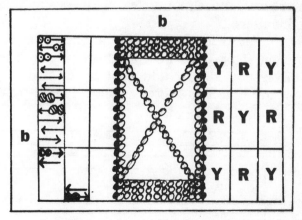

○   *White*   ☉   *Mustard Yellow*
⊕   *Rose*   Y   *Mustard Yellow*
●   *Trans Dark Blue*   R   *Rose*
b   *Dark Blue Border*

Figure 9-20

83

GEOMETRIC PATTERN BEADED BELT

Materials

1	Red Wool Piece - 30 1/8" x 4"
1	White Muslin Piece - 31" x 4"
1	Medium Weight Cowhide Piece - 34" x 2 3/4"
16	Brass Spots - 3/8"
1	Buckskin Thong - 15" long
1	Spool Cotton Sewing Thread - Size 16
1	Bobbin Nylon Beading Thread - Size A
5	Hanks Size 12/° Seed Beads:
	1 Yellow, 2 White &
	2 Transparent Cobalt Blue

The simple, bold colors and broad geometric patterns in this piece are commonly found in older Northern Plains beadwork. A belt such as this would have been favored by men. Beaded belts represent a great deal of work and are saved for special occasions. They are worn with decorated belt accessories and one's best clothes.

SIZING

The belt described in this chapter is a size 34, but it can easily be adjusted to a larger or smaller size. This decision must be made before assembling the materials however, as the lengths of the wool, muslin, and leather pieces may need to be altered.

The belt can be made a size 32 or 31 by cutting 2 or 3 inches off the cowhide blank. Conversely, simply add an inch or two to the cowhide blank to increase the belt size by that amount.

For greater size differences, the beadwork and the other materials must also be changed. If the belt is shortened greatly, delete the last square in the pattern at each end of the beadwork and shorten the wool and muslin by 3 inches. Shorten the cowhide as needed. With the same theory in mind, if the belt is made significantly longer, add an extra square to each end of the beadwork. In this case, two extra brass spots will

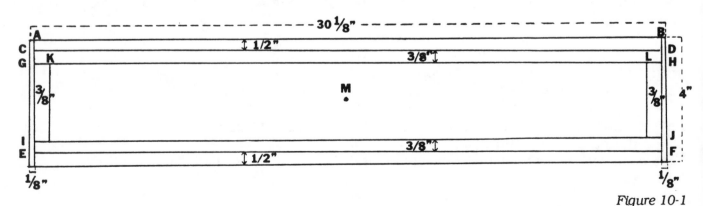

Figure 10-1

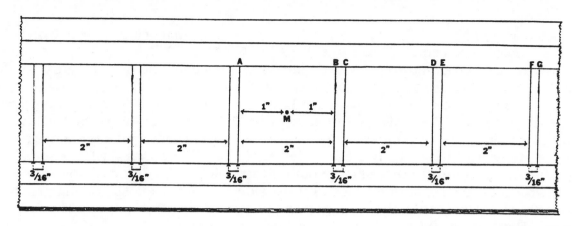

Figure 10-2

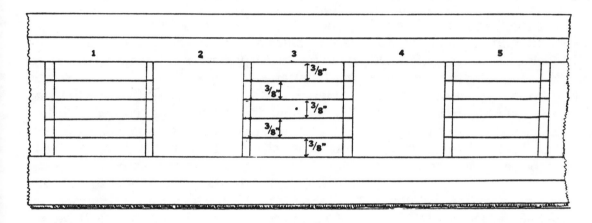

Figure 10-3

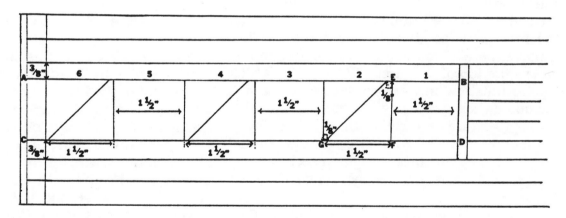

Figure 10-4

be needed and 3 inches will have to be added to the wool and muslin. Increase the length of the cowhide blank as needed.

LAYOUT

The beadwork on this piece is done on the 30 1/8 x 4 inch piece of red wool. Use a marking pen and draw the border lines shown in Figure 10-1 on the wool. Start with vertical lines A and B, which are located 1/8 inch from the ends of the cloth. Then draw two horizontal lines; line C-D is 1/2 inch from the top edge of the wool and line E-F is 1/2 inch from the bottom edge. Lines G-H and I-J are parallel to the last two lines. Draw them 3/8 inch inside lines C-D and E-F respectively; this set of lines marks the upper and lower limits of the main beading area. The final border lines are vertical lines K and L. Draw them 3/8 inch from lines A and B and run them between

85

lines G-H and I-J.

Locate the center of the strip of wool and place a small mark there (point M in Figure 10-1). To do this, find the halfway point between the top and bottom on each end and lay a ruler between these two points. The center is the midway point on the ruler.

Now draw the beading areas in the center of the belt, working inside the border outline just drawn. Begin by measuring 1 inch to either side of point M. Draw a vertical line at each point (lines A and B in Figure 10-2), creating a 2 inch square in the center of the belt. Make another vertical line (C) 3/16 inch to the right of line B. Move another 2 inches to the right and draw line D. Continue with line E, 3/16 inch further to the right. Draw line F, 2 inches to the right of line E and line G, another 3/16 inch to the right.

Go back to line A and begin measuring in the same pattern to the left (see Figure 10-2). Add five vertical lines in this direction, alternating 3/16 and 2 inches apart. This will result in five squares in the center of the belt, each bordered by 3/16 inch spaces.

In the center square, start 3/8 inch down from the top and mark four points, 3/8 inch apart, down the left edge (Figure 10-3). The squares are numbered 1 to 5, from left to right so the center square is number 3. Place a ruler on the first point so that it runs across all five squares, parallel to the horizontal lines running across the top of the piece. Start in the far left square and draw lines across squares 1, 3, and 5, including their 3/16 inch borders. Repeat this same procedure at the other three points, dividing squares 1, 3, and 5 into five equal, horizontal rows. To keep the lines straight, a second set of marks may be made on the edge of one of the other squares.

Draw the beading areas on the ends of the wool next. Begin on the left, next to the central section just completed. Draw a horizontal line 3/8 inch below the top line of the main beading section (line A-B in Figure 10-4). Draw a second line (C-D) 3/8 inch above the bottom line of this section. Divide the area between these two lines into six rectangles, each 1 1/2 inches wide. Start by measuring 1 1/2 inches to the left of line B-D and drawing a vertical line (E-F). The next line is drawn 1 1/2 inches to the left of line E-F, and so on until all six rectangles have been drawn. These are numbered 1 to 6, from right to left, in Figure 10-4.

Draw diagonal lines in rectangles 2, 4 and 6 from the top right corner to the bottom left corner. These lines should be set in from the vertical sides of the corners by 1/8 inch, to allow room for the vertical rows of beadwork which will run between each square (see line E-G in square 2, Figure 10-4). Once this beadwork is in place, the diagonal line will run from corner to corner.

Draw another six rectangles on the right end of the belt. Use the same procedure and work from the center section towards the end. Reverse the direction of the diagonal lines in squares 2, 4 and 6 so that the lines run from the upper left corner to the lower right corner of each square. Offset these lines 1/8 inch from the corners.

BEADING INSTRUCTIONS

Check the layout against Figure 10-5 before beginning the beadwork. Start in the upper left corner of the border outline, on the second line from the top of the wool (point A). Use transparent cobalt blue beads and bead across the top of the belt to the upper right corner of the outline (point B) with a Three Bead Return Stitch. Continue down the right edge of the outline to point C, on the second line from the bottom. Finally, bead back across the belt on this line to the left edge of the outline (point D). Bead up the

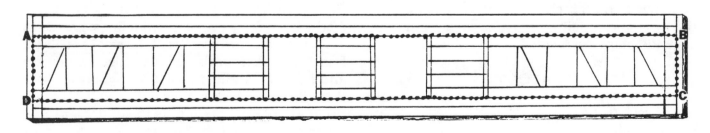

● *Transparent Cobalt Blue*

Figure 10-5

86

Figure 10-6

○ *White*   ● *Cobalt Blue*   ⊙ *Yellow*

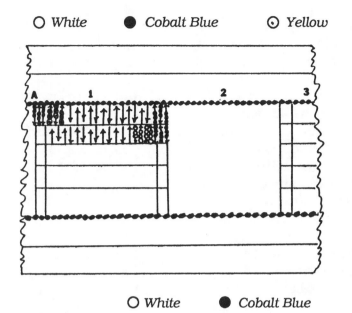

left side from point D back to point A. This row of beading marks the outside edge of the main beadwork area and is referred to in these directions as the main blue outline.

Next bead the three large squares located in the center of the belt, which were divided into horizontal rows. Start in the upper left corner of the square on the left, designated number 1 in the layout instructions (point A in Figure 10-6). Use a Lazy Stitch and work towards the right side of the square, beading back and forth between the horizontal guidelines. Bead the edges of the square, marked by the lines which are 3/16 inch apart, with cobalt blue beads, which should take about three stitches on each end. The main color area of each square alternates by row from yellow to white. Bead the top row of the first square with yellow beads from left to right, the next row down with white beads from right to left, and so on until the 5th row is completed. Remember to maintain the outside border of cobalt blue beads in each row.

Leave square 2 blank, using the red wool as part of the design, and bead square 3 (the center square). Again use a Lazy Stitch and bead the right

Figure 10-7

○ *White*   ● *Cobalt Blue*   ⊙ *Yellow*

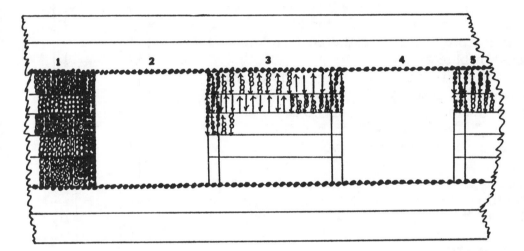

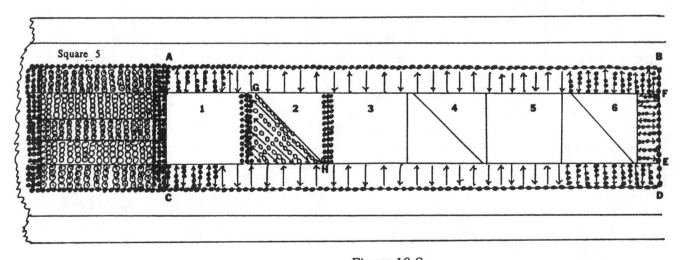

Figure 10-8

○ *White*   ● *Cobalt Blue*   ⊙ *Yellow*

and left edges in blue. Alternate the row colors from white to yellow, starting with white in the top row (Figure 10-7).

Leave square 4 blank and continue beading in square 5. Bead square 5 in the exact same manner as square 1. Maintain the blue border on both edges and use yellow for the main color in the first row (see Figures 10-6 and 10-7).

Bead the right end of the belt next. Begin by Lazy Stitching with transparent cobalt blue beads back and forth between the main blue outline and the top of the small rectangles in this section (Figure 10-8). Start to the right of the central beadwork just completed (point A) and work across to the right end of the main blue outline (point B). Repeat this procedure on the row between the bottom of the rectangles and the main blue outline, working from point C to point D. Complete this Lazy Stitch border by beading from point E to point F between the end of the small rectangles and the main outline.

Bead the vertical border of each of the small rectangles on this end of the belt with blue beads. Use three rows of blue beads on each of the borders as shown in Figure 10-8. Start at the top and use a Three Bead Return Stitch, beading directly on the line to the bottom. Move to the right and bead a second row from the bottom to the top. Then move to the left of the first row and bead a third row from the top to the bottom. Do this on each of the five vertical lines marked on the wool, ending with six small rectangles bordered by blue beads.

Rectangles 2, 4, and 6 are divided in half by a diagonal line in each square. Bead the left half of each of these squares in white with a Three Bead Return Stitch. Begin in the top left corner (point G in Figure 10-8) and bead on the diagonal line to the bottom right corner (point H). Fill the area below this row by beading back and forth, parallel to the first row of beads. Bead all three rectangles in this manner.

Bead the left end of the belt in the same manner as the right end, except that the right half of the rectangles divided by the diagonal line should be beaded instead of the left.

CONSTRUCTION

The belt is now ready to sew together. Begin by folding the ends of the wool piece under along the edge of the beaded area (Figure 10-9). Center the beaded wool on top of the leather belt blank. Use a Running Stitch and a Glover's needle with heavy cotton thread to sew across the top and bottom of the belt, just outside the beadwork. Stitch completely through the wool and leather.

Sew the folded ends of the wool to the leather blank in the same manner. Sew extremely close to the beadwork, so that the stitches are almost hidden by the beads (Figure 10-10). Trim the top and bottom edges of the wool even with the edges of the leather belt blank.

Put the brass spots on the belt next. First make a small mark in the center of each blank red square or rectangle with a marking pen. The best way to find the center is by eye; absolute accuracy is unnecessary in this step of the work.

The brass spots have four prongs on the back which must go completely through the wool and the leather. The prongs are not strong or sharp enough to push through the leather, so four small slots must

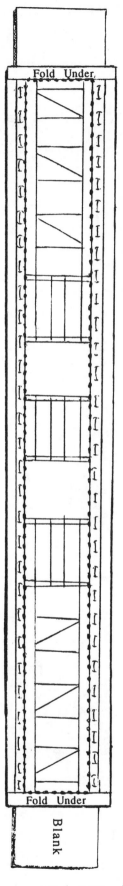

Transparent Cobalt Blue ●

Figure 10-9

Figure 10-10

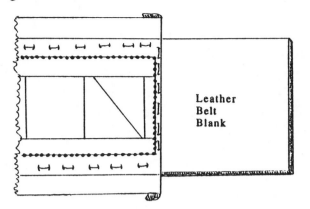

Leather
Belt
Blank

Figure 10-11

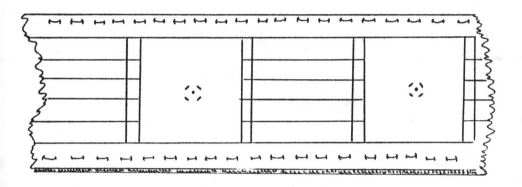

Figure 10-12

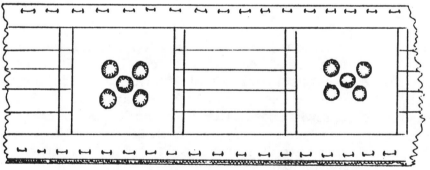

of the belt have five brass spots each; one in the center and four around the central one as shown in Figure 10-12. Arrange the other four spots around the central one, at a distance of about 1/4 inch, and attach them in the same manner as the previous ones.

Take the strip of muslin, which is used to back the beaded portion of the belt, and fold over about 1/2 inch of the cloth along the top edge and one of the ends (Figure 10-13).

Place the muslin under the belt with the folds facing the back of the belt. The folded end of the muslin should just cover the end stitching on the back of the leather and the long folded edge should be at the top of the belt (Figure 10-14).

Fold the top edge of the muslin again, bringing it over the top edge of the belt by about 1/4 inch. Pin the muslin to the top edge of the red wool, making sure to keep the cut or raw edge of the muslin folded under. Place the pins parallel to the top edge of the belt and space them about an inch apart.

Fold the second end of the muslin towards the belt so that it too just covers the end stitching on the back of the leather. Finally, fold the raw bottom edge of the muslin up about 1/2 inch and then wrap this folded edge around the bottom edge of the belt. Pull the muslin snug around the back of the belt and pin the bottom edge to the red wool in the same manner as was done on the top edge.

Using the beading needle and thread, Whip Stitch the muslin to the red wool along the top and bottom edges (Figure 10-15).

Turn the belt over and stitch the ends of the muslin to the leather on the back of the belt (Figure 10-16). Use a Whip Stitch and beading thread as before.

Punch four medium size holes in each of the leather ends of the belt. The holes should be about 5/8 inch apart and run in a vertical line 1/2 inch from the edge of the leather. These holes are to lace the 15 inch buckskin thong through

be cut for them with a craft blade or other small sharp knife. To position the cuts, press the brass spot firmly on the wool over the mark in the center of each red square. Lift the spot off the wool and make the cuts on the marks left by each of the prongs (Figure 10-11).

Push the prongs through the cuts in the wool and leather. Fold them over toward the center of the spot by tapping them with a small tack hammer. The prongs should be flush with the surface of the leather; imbedding them in the leather can cause a pucker in the finished belt.

The large red squares in the center section

Figure 10-13

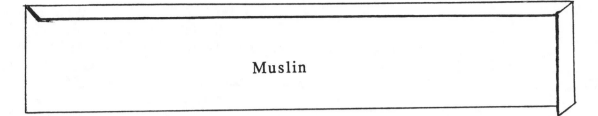

Muslin

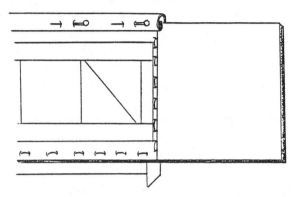

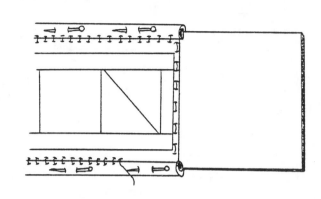

Figure 10-14   Figure 10-15

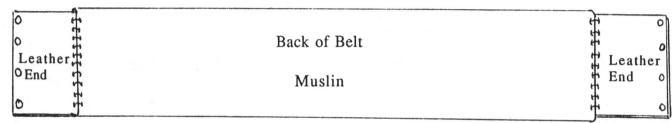

Back of Belt

Muslin

Leather End

Leather End

Figure 10-16

and they must line up with each other, so that the edges of the belt will be even when the belt is tied on. One way to do this is to punch the holes in one end, then wrap the belt in a circle and align the ends. Mark the locations of the holes on the unpunched end and punch the new holes even with these marks.

BEADED EDGING

Finish the top and bottom edges of this belt with a Lazy Stitch zigzag pattern in blue and white. The beading pattern for this edging is graphed in Figure 10-17. The graph is divided into three sections because of the length of the belt but there are no breaks in beading between these sections. The edging in the graph is eight beads wide, however the beads should extend from the main blue outline to the edge of the belt. Adjust the number of beads as necessary to match the exact width of the belt. Note that the edging must be at least six beads wide to accom-

modate the pattern. Also keep in mind that the number of bead rows (stitches) in each of the sections is approximate as the spacing between stitches may vary enough to change the number of rows needed. The letters marked on the graph correspond to the letters in Figure 10-18. Use these two diagrams to aid in placing the pattern on the belt.

Begin the beadwork in the lower left corner of the center square (point B). This is the first row of all blue beads in the graph. Do not wrap the beads around the edge of the belt as there is too much wear on the back of a belt. If the beads or stitching carry over to the back, the thread will break quite easily from the strain. Lazy Stitch towards the left end of the belt, decreasing the number of blue beads in each successive row (stitch) by one until there is only one blue bead at the top of the row. The number of white beads in each stitch will, of course, increase as the number of blue beads decreases.

Begin the zigzag or sawtooth pattern at

90

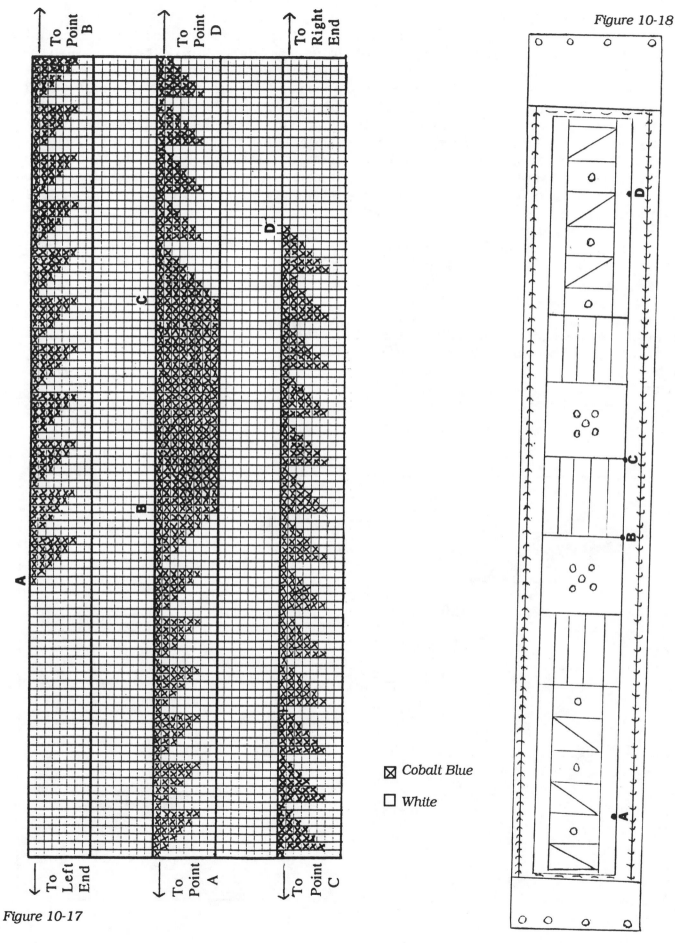

To Point B

To Point D

To Right End

A

C

B

D

To Left End

To Point A

To Point C

Figure 10-17

Figure 10-18

D

C

B

A

⊠ Cobalt Blue

☐ White

91

this point. As the graph shows, put six blue beads in the next row, then decrease the number of blue beads in each subsequent row by one again until there is only one blue bead at the top of the stitch. Continue in this manner to the bottom left corner of the 4th small rectangle from the center (point A). Once this point is reached, complete the sawtooth in progress, then bead the remainder of the belt to the left with rows of white beads. There should be about 17 sawtooth patterns.

Return to point B and work the edging towards the right end of the belt. Add rows made entirely of blue beads to the bottom right corner of the center square (point C). From there decrease the number of blue beads in each of the following rows by one until there is only one blue bead in the row. Begin the sawtooth pattern as before by putting six blue beads in the top of the next row. Use the same procedure as on the left end of the belt and bead the sawtooth pattern out to the bottom right corner of the 4th square from the center of the belt (point D). Again, complete the sawtooth pattern in progress, then bead to the end of the belt with rows of white beads.

Turn the belt upside down and repeat the same edging procedure on the bottom of the belt. The sawtooths on this edge will point in the opposite direction from the ones on the bottom edge.

Lace the buckskin thong through the holes in the ends of the belt to tie it on. Crisscross the thong through the holes working from the top of the belt to the bottom (Figure 10-19). The tie is most often worn in the back.

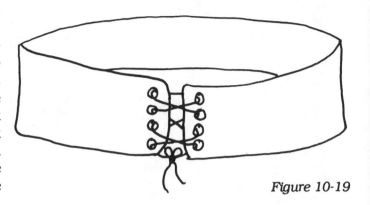

Figure 10-19

FLORAL BEADED BELT

Materials
1   Buckskin Piece - 31" x 3"
1   White Muslin Piece - 33" x 4"
1   Medium Weight Cowhide Piece - 31" x 2 3/4"
1   Buckskin Thong - 15" long
1   Spool Cotton Sewing Thread - Size 16
1   Bobbin Nylon Beading Thread - Size A
10   Hanks Size 12/° Seed Beads:
2 White, 1 Transparent Medium Blue,
1 Transparent Dark Green, 1 Transparent Pink,
1 Transparent Grey, 1 Transparent Dark Red,
1 Transparent Gold, 1 Lavender & 1 Greasy White
1   Tube Barge Cement

This piece is intricately beaded and should not be attempted by beginning beadworkers. There are many places in the design where judgement and experience in bead placement are needed to decide on the addition or subtraction of a single bead. These decisions can be crucial to the integrity of the design and to the ultimate beauty of the piece.

A completely beaded belt, especially one this intricate, is a very special piece and is usually saved for important occasions. The floral pattern on this belt shows Eastern and Canadian influences and the colors indicate it was styled after fairly early beadwork.

SIZING

The belt described in this chapter is a size 30. It can easily be made larger or smaller by adding to or subtracting from the length of the buckskin, muslin, and cowhide pieces before beginning. Obviously, this decision must be made before assembling the materials. If the size of the belt is greatly altered, the distances between the elements of the floral beading pattern will need to be squeezed together or spread apart.

LAYOUT

The beadwork on this piece is done on the 31 by 3 inch strip of buckskin. Find the center of this strip and mark it with a pen (point A in Figure 11-1).

Measure 7 1/2 inches to the left of point A,

along an imaginary center line on the leather, and make another mark (point B). Make one more mark (point C), 7 1/2 inches to the right of point A.

Now draw the border guidelines for the main area of the beadwork. First, measure 7/8 inch from either end of the leather and draw two vertical lines. They should run from 1/4 inch below the top edge to 1/4 inch above the bottom edge (see Figure 11-1). Connect these vertical lines with horizontal lines running 1/4 inch from the top and bottom edges of the buckskin.

Draw the four floral patterns on the leather in the manner described below. This pattern is provided in Figure 11-2 on a grid where one square is equal to one square inch.

Begin by measuring 1 1/4 inches to the

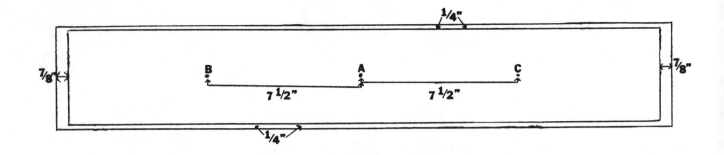

Figure 11-1

Figure 11-2

right of point A and making a small mark (point D in Figure 11-3). Draw a horizontal figure eight with point D at its center and loops which are about 7/16 inch long and 1/4 inch across at their widest points. These loops form the two side petals in the center of the flower. Make a similar horizontal figure eight with point C at its center.

Repeat this procedure to the left of point A, drawing two more horizontal figure eights. The first should be centered on a point 1 1/4 inches to the left of point A and the second should be centered on point B.

Next draw four vertical figure eights, centering them on each of the four points described above. Finish drawing the four flowers by adding the middle and outer sets of petals as shown in Figure 11-2. Use the grid squares as a reference for the size and spacing of the petals.

Now draw the bottom section of the leaf portion of the design for each of the floral patterns. To position the leaf section correctly, draw

the center vein of this bottom portion first (Figure 11-4). Again, use the grid in Figure 11-2 and a ruler to determine the correct length and curve of this line. Note that the veins on the left side of the belt are a mirror image of the pattern and must be reversed. Add the short lines shown in Figure 11-4 to the center veins on each of the four floral patterns.

The remaining leaf parts on the bottom should now be easy to draw, using the short lines as a guide. Draw the leaf segments below the center vein first, then draw the segments above the vein.

When these are completed for each of the floral patterns, draw the top curved lines of each leaf section. Start close to the flower with the lower of the two guidelines (Figure 11-5). Note that this line reaches its lowest point at the tip of the third or middle leaf segment above the center vein on the bottom, then sweeps up to a curled tip. Draw the line which branches up and to the

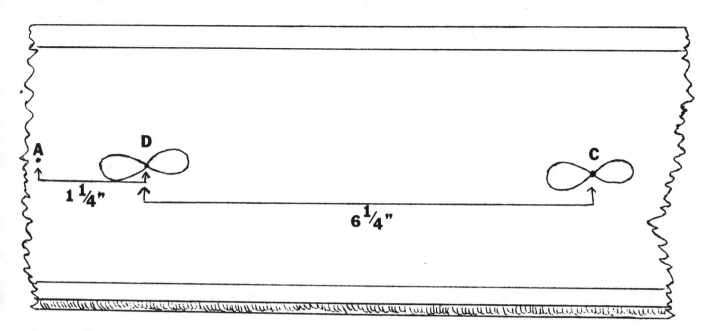

Figure 11-3

Figure 11-4

Figure 11-6

Figure 11-5

right of this tip next.

    Finally draw the uppermost line. Follow the curve of the lower line as shown in Figure 11-2, then come around the tips of the lower line and join the bottom section at the tip of the second bottom leaf segment. The small spike leaves at the tops of the flowers will be drawn later.

BEADING INSTRUCTIONS

    The beadwork in this pattern follows the same sequence as the layout. Start in the center of the flowers and work section by section from the center petals to the outer petals. Begin with the horizontal figure eight in the flower at the left end of the belt. Use transparent dark red beads and a Two Bead Return Stitch. Start just to the right of the center (point A in Figure 11-6) and bead around the outside edge in a figure eight as shown.

    Return to the center of the figure eight, inside the petal on the right (see Figure 11-6). Run a second row of dark red beads around the

Figure 11-7

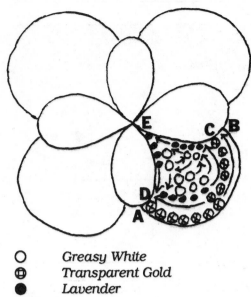

○   *Greasy White*
⊕   *Transparent Gold*
●   *Lavender*

Figure 11-8

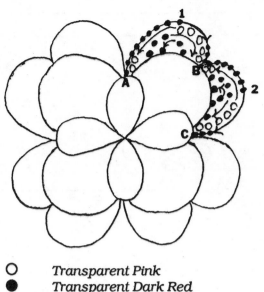

○   *Transparent Pink*
●   *Transparent Dark Red*

Firgure 11-9

petal, inside the previous row. Fill the remainder of the petal with rows of transparent grey beads which follow the curve of the dark red rows.

Move to the petal on the left of the figure eight and repeat this procedure to fill the area. Then move to the vertical figure eight and bead it with the same techniques and colors (Figure 11-7). Repeat all these steps in the central portions of each of the three remaining flowers.

Bead the middle set of petals in each of the flowers next. Again, start with the flower at the left end of the belt. Place the first row of beading in the petal on the lower right side of the flower.

Use a Two Bead Return Stitch and start on the bottom left edge of the petal (point A in Figure 11-8). Use transparent gold beads and run the first row along the outer edge to point B at the top, right of the petal. Run a second row of transparent gold beads inside the first, from point C to point D.

Move to point E, as close to the center of the flower as possible, and bead a row of lavender beads down to point D. Continue around the petal, just inside the rows of gold beads, with lavender beads to the top of the petal by point C. From there bead back along the top edge to point

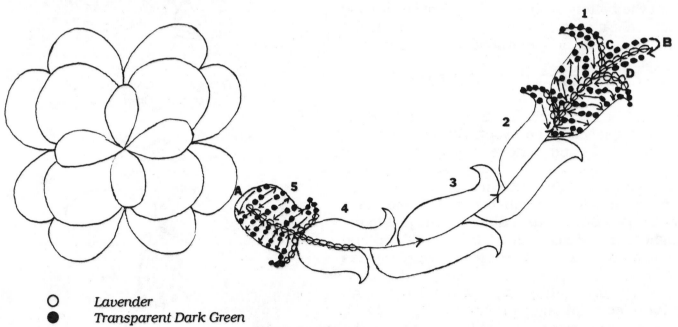

○   *Lavender*
●   *Transparent Dark Green*

Figure 11-10

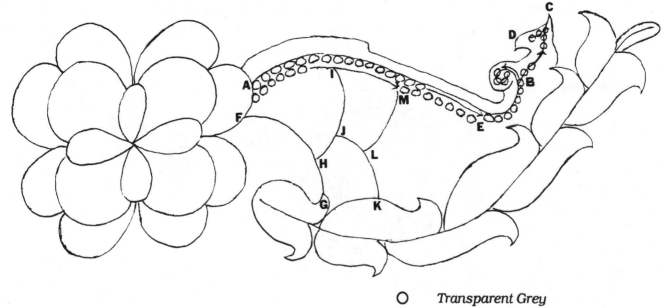

○   *Transparent Grey*

Figure 11-11

E. Switch to greasy white beads and bead a row inside the lavender row just completed. Fill the remaining area in this petal with greasy white beads. Bead back and forth in an arc, working from the center out as shown in Figure 11-8. Repeat these steps in each of the four middle petals on this flower and then bead the middle petals of the other three flowers in the same fashion.

The beading scheme for the outside set of petals is shown in Figure 11-9. Use a Three Bead Return Stitch and stitch a row of dark red beads from point A, at the top center of the flower, clockwise around the outside edge of the first petal. This edge intersects the middle petals at point B. Continue with the same color and stitch around the second outside petal to its intersection with the center petals at point C.

Bead a row of transparent pink, inside the dark red row, from point C back to point B. Switch to a Two Bead Return Stitch and fill the remainder of the second petal with rows of dark red beads, going back and forth inside the curve of the earlier rows.

Move back to the first petal and bead it in the same manner, starting with a row of transparent pink beads from point B to point A. Fill the rest of the petal with dark red beads. Repeat these steps in the other outside petals on this flower and then in the outside petals on each of the other three flowers.

Bead the bottom sections of the leaf pat-

terns next. Start with the pattern on the right side of the belt and bead the center vein with a Three Bead Return Stitch and lavender beads. Begin at point A, next to the flower, and bead out to the tip at point B (Figure 11-10). When the end of the vein is reached, take a series of small stitches in the buckskin above the center vein, moving the thread down to the intersection of the first side vein (point C). Switch to transparent dark green beads and bead around the tip of the leaf, past point B, to the intersection of the first side vein below the center vein (point D).

Now bead the leaf segments. Use a Three Bead Return Stitch as much as possible. However, as the segments narrow it may be necessary to decrease the number of beads per stitch. Each leaf segment has two halves, one above the center vein and one below it. Begin in the segment nearest the tip of the leaf, in the half above the center vein. This segment is labelled number 1 in Figure 11-10. Bead from the junction of the top edge with the center vein (point C), out to the tip of the leaf segment. The first four or five beads in this row are lavender and the rest are dark green. The lavender beads create a small side vein and are used on the top edges of each leaf segment.

Take a small stitch in the buckskin at the end of the first row and reverse the direction of stitching. Bead a second row, using all dark green beads, back towards the center vein. Continue to bead back and forth with rows of dark green beads until this portion of the leaf segment

97

Figure 11-12

○ Transparent Grey
● Transparent Medium Blue
⊕ Lavender

○ Transparent Pink
● Transparent Dark Green
⊕ Lavender

Figure 11-13

is filled.

Repeat this beading procedure in the half of this leaf segment which is below the center vein. Remember to put four or five lavender beads in the row along the top edge. Move down the center vein, beading each of the succeeding leaf segments in the same manner until the last segment is reached.

The last leaf segment, marked number 5 in Figure 11-10, is beaded slightly differently from the rest. Begin with the portion above the center vein and bead it in the same manner as the rest until the bottom of the center vein is reached. At this point extend the stitching all the way across the leaf segment for a row or two until the end guideline is reached. Then move to the top edge of the portion below the center vein and bead it exactly like the others.

Repeat these steps in the bottom leaf sections of the remaining three floral patterns.

Figure 11-14

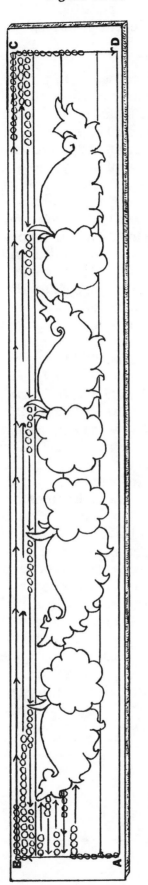

Figure 11-15

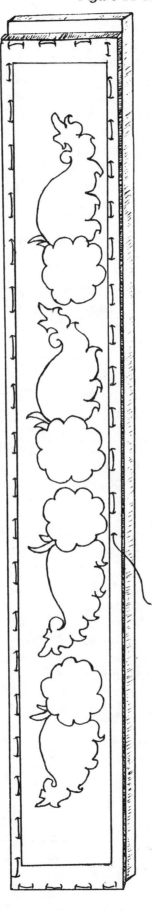

Figure 11-16

Move to the upper part of the leaf in the floral pattern on the right side of the belt. Start just below the lower of the two lines at the top, next to the flower (point A in Figure 11-11). Use a Three Bead Return Stitch and bead a row of transparent gray from point A to point B, where the guideline branches. At point B, switch to a Two Bead Return Stitch and bead on the curving line to the left, going around the curlicue on the end.

Return to point B and continue with gray beads up the right branch of the line to its tip at point C. Bead on top of the guideline. Reverse direction by taking a small stitch in the leather at point C and run the line of gray beads out the small side branch to the left, ending at its tip (point D).

Return to point A and run a second row of gray beads across the top of the leaf pattern, beneath the first row. Bead across to point E, which is located several beads to the left of the tip of the third leaf segment on the bottom.

Again, repeat these steps on the other three floral patterns.

Next, four lines must be drawn to delineate the scale-like design in each of the four leaves. Refer to Figure 11-11 while drawing these lines. Draw the first line from point F to point G; point F is located just below point A on the top right of the flower and point G is located at the tip of leaf segment 5. Draw the next line from point H to point I; point H is in the center of line F-G and point I is just below the rows of gray beads, about a third of the way between points A and E. Draw the third line from point J to point K; point J is in the center of line H-I and point K is in the middle of leaf segment 4. Draw the last line from point L to point M; point L is in the middle of line J-K and point M is below the rows of gray beads, about two thirds of the way between points A and E.

Bead these scale designs next; the beading pattern for these sections is given in Figure 11-12. Use a Three Bead Return Stitch and start at point F. Bead a row of gray beads on top of the guideline from point F down to point G. Bead a second row of gray, inside the first, from point G back to point F. Change to transparent medium blue beads and continue to run rows of beads back and forth inside the gray rows. Work towards the flower and fill this space completely.

Move to point H and bead a row of gray beads on top of the guideline from point H to point I (see Figure 11-11 for point locations). At point I, reverse the direction of the stitching and bead a second row of gray, inside the first, back to point H. Switch to transparent medium blue beads and fill the area of the second scale by working rows back and forth towards the flower in the same fashion as before. Bead the two remaining scales in a similar manner, working the first row of the third scale from point J to point K and the first row of the 4th scale from point L to point M.

Still using Figure 11-12, move to point A at the top of the leaf pattern. Use a Three Bead Return Stitch and stitch a row of lavender beads above the top row of gray beads, from point A to point B. Reverse direction and stitch a second row, just above the first, back to point A. Reverse direction once more at point N, which is at the upper guideline next to the flower. Run a third row of lavender beads from point N to point O at the top of the curve on the leaf. Move to point P where the top section joins the bottom section. Use lavender beads and bead around the upper tip of the pattern and along the upper edge; when the curlicue is reached, bead around it, leaving

the outside edge and beading back towards point B as far as possible.

Repeat these steps on the other three floral patterns.

Fill the remainder of all four leaves with rows of transparent pink beads (Figure 11-13). Use a Three Bead Return Stitch where possible, but the small curves in this section will quite often require a change in the number of beads per stitch. Begin at point A, which is at the end of the inner row of gray beads. Bead just below the outer row of gray beads towards point B, near the tip of the upper leaf section. Go as far as possible, then reverse direction and bead a second row from point B back to point C, which is below the inner row of gray at the end of the scale section.

Complete the main fill work with rows of pink beads which follow the upper contour of the leaf, running back and forth between the scales and the bottom leaf segments (see Figure 11-13). When this main fill is completed, return to the tip of the leaf and fill the open areas, if any remain. Start along the top edge of leaf segment 3 (point D) and bead back and forth between point D and the tip of the leaf (point B) to fill this space.

Draw the small spike leaves at the top of each flower next to the leaf pattern. Refer back to the pattern in Figure 11-2 and make sure that the leaves are wide enough to accommodate three rows of beads for most of their length. The beading pattern for these leaves is shown in Figure 11-13. Start in the bottom, right corner of the larger spike (point E) with transparent dark green beads and a Two Bead Return Stitch. Bead up to the tip of the spike at point F. At the tip, reverse direction with a small stitch in the leather and continue beading with dark green beads down to point G. Add a row of lavender beads between these two dark green rows.

Move to the shorter spike and repeat this procedure. Begin the first row of green at point G, bead up to the tip of the spike at point H, and then

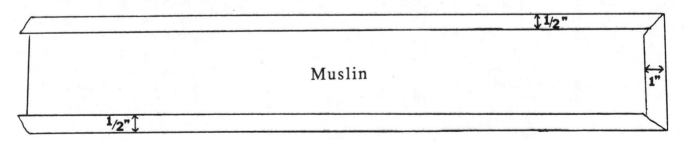

Muslin

$1/2$"

$1/2$"

1"

Figure 11-17

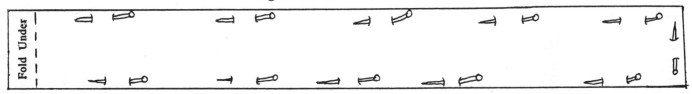

Figure 11-18

stitch down the other side of the leaf to point I. Stitch a row of lavender beads up the middle of this spike as well. Bead all four leaf patterns in this manner.

Move to the background area of the belt and draw three guidelines all the way across the belt, skipping the beaded areas as necessary (Figure 11-14). The actual position of the lines is not critical, but they must run straight across the belt. These lines will act as guides to prevent crooked rows when the background is beaded, as there is a great tendency for the rows to slope up or down as the work progresses.

Use white beads for the entire background and, as much as possible, use a Three Bead Return Stitch. Once again, the number of beads per stitch will vary as the background is worked around the floral patterns. Outline three sides of the main beading area before beginning the fill work. Start in the lower left corner (point A in Figure 11-15) and bead up to the top left corner (point B). Continue beading across the top guideline to the upper right corner (point C), then down to the lower right corner (point D). Leave the bottom guideline unbeaded at this time to allow for slight adjustments in the bottom rows.

Return to the top left corner (point B) and begin to fill the background by beading across the top of the belt again to point C. Continue stitching rows of beads back and forth across the top of the belt. Skip places where the rows run into the floral patterns, as long as the patches of floral beadwork remain fairly small (see Figure 11-15). When the background fill runs into the main part of the design, begin beading back and forth between the end of the belt and the design. Stop at the bottom of the main part of the floral pattern.

Go back and fill the spaces between and around the floral patterns in this middle section of the belt. Beading these areas in sections from top to bottom is faster than trying to continue all the way across the belt and makes it easier to keep the rows running straight.

When all the small areas around the pattern have been filled, begin beading all the way

across the belt again, below the main part of the floral pattern. When the entire belt is filled, stitch a last row of white beads across the guideline at the bottom of the belt.

CONSTRUCTION

The belt can now be constructed. First, center the beaded leather strip on the cowhide blank and glue the two pieces together with barge cement. Place the two strips under several books to keep them flat and pressed tightly together. Leave them overnight to allow the glue to dry. The next day, trim the top and bottom edges of the glued buckskin and cowhide to about 3/8 inch from the beadwork. Trim the short edges on the end even with one another, but leave them as long as possible.

Sew the cowhide to the buckskin with a Glover's needle, heavy cotton thread and a Running Stitch. Stitch next to the beadwork on the top and bottom edges, but continue beyond the beadwork to the ends of the belt and stitch them together on the far edges (Figure 11-16). Be careful not to cut any of the beading threads with the Glover's needle.

Prepare to stitch the muslin backing to the belt by folding about 1/2 inch of fabric over on the top and bottom edges and about 1 inch of fabric on one of the ends (Figure 11-17). Make sure that the muslin is slightly larger than the belt in all directions, as it must wrap up over the edges of the belt and be stitched to the buckskin on the front.

Center the muslin from top to bottom on the back of the belt, with the raw edges folded between the two pieces, and the folded end just beyond the end of the belt. Pin the folded edges of the muslin to the back of the belt (Figure 11-18). Then fold under the last raw edge of the muslin so that the end is just beyond the end of the belt and pin it to the back of the belt.

Wrap the edges of the muslin around to the front of the belt and Whip Stitch them to the buckskin (Figure 11-19). Use the beading needle

101

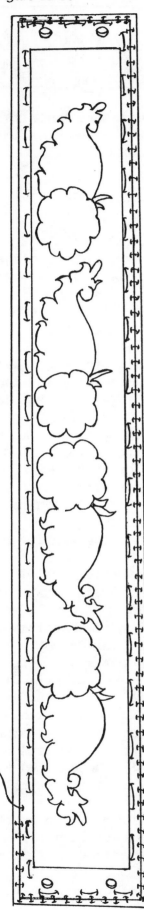

Figure 11-19

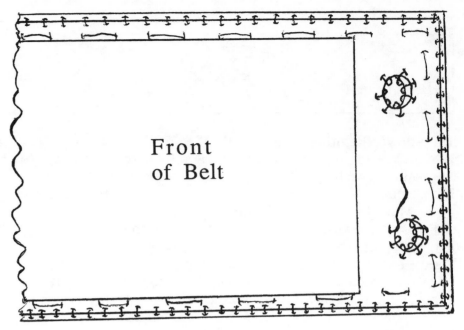

Front
of Belt

Figure 11-20

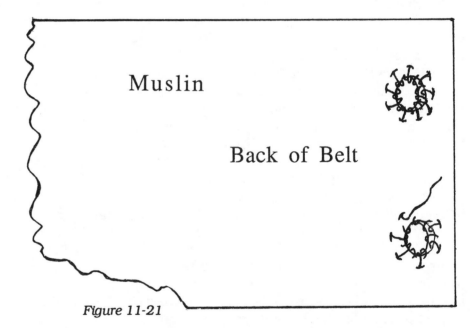

Muslin

Back of Belt

Figure 11-21

and thread and stitch down all four edges.

Punch two holes in each end of the belt, through all the thicknesses of leather and fabric. Use the largest awl available on the leather punch and position the holes about 1/2 inch from the edge of the leather. Make sure that the holes on one end line up with the holes on the other end, so that the edges of the belt will be even when the belt is tied.

Bind these tie holes with Whip Stitching, still using the beading needle and thread. Begin on the front of the belt and stitch all the way around each hole, through all three thicknesses of leather and fabric (Figure 11-20). Turn the belt over and stitch the muslin to the cowhide around the holes, again using a Whip Stitch (Figure 11-21). Keep these stitches very close together and be sure that enough fabric is caught in each stitch to prevent it from unravelling as the leather thong passes in and out of the holes.

FINAL BEADING

Use a Three Bead Return Stitch and transparent medium blue beads to stitch a single row around the edge of the belt. On the top and bottom edges, run the blue beads along the outside row of white beads. On the ends of the belt, stitch the blue beads along the edge of the leather (Figure 11-22).

Add a row of blue beads around each of the tie holes.

Figure 11-22

Use a Two Bead Return Stitch as this is a very tight curve. Fill in the remaining areas at the ends of the belt. Use medium blue beads and a Three Bead Return Stitch. Stitch the rows vertically between the top and bottom of the belt. As before, the number of beads per stitch will vary as the beads are worked around the tie holes.

Run the leather thong through the tie holes. Tie the belt by lacing the thong through the holes like a shoe lace (Figure 11-23). Wear the belt with the tie in the back and place a ration ticket bag over the tie.

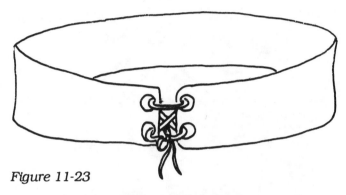

Figure 11-23

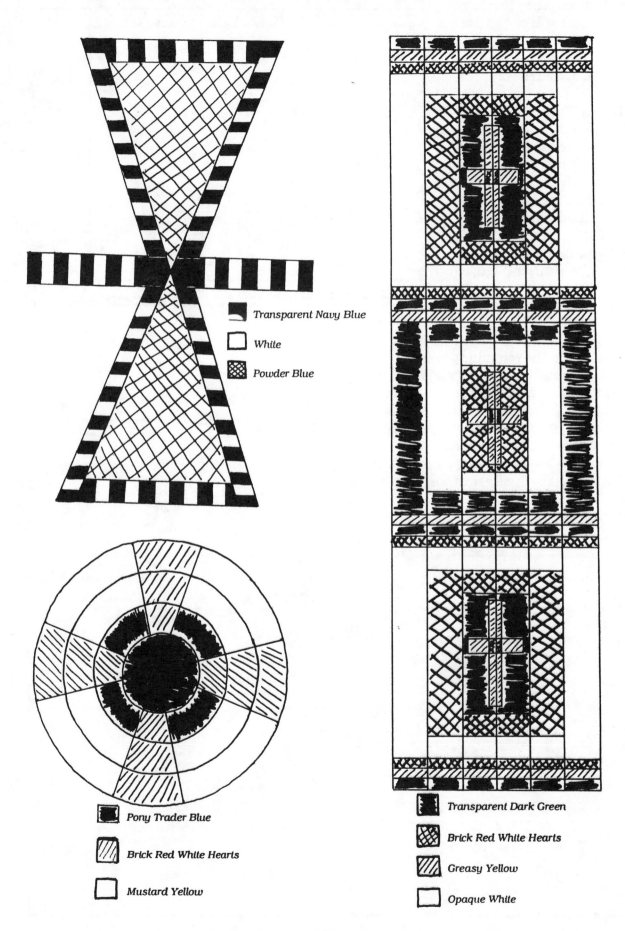

Transparent Navy Blue

White

Powder Blue

Pony Trader Blue

Brick Red White Hearts

Mustard Yellow

Transparent Dark Green

Brick Red White Hearts

Greasy Yellow

Opaque White

104

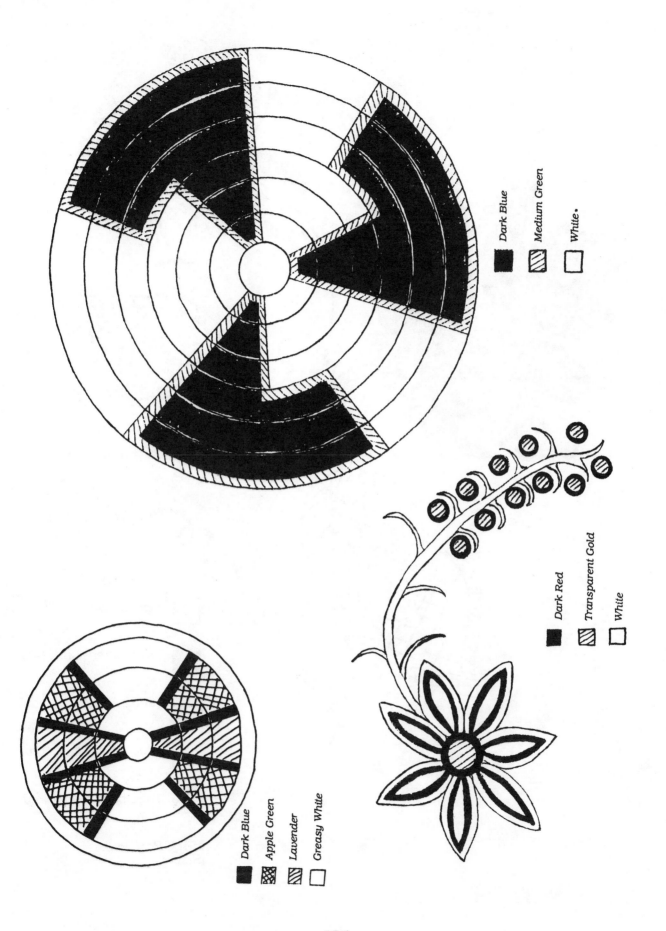

Dark Blue

Medium Green

White.

Dark Red

Transparent Gold

White

Dark Blue

Apple Green

Lavender

Greasy White

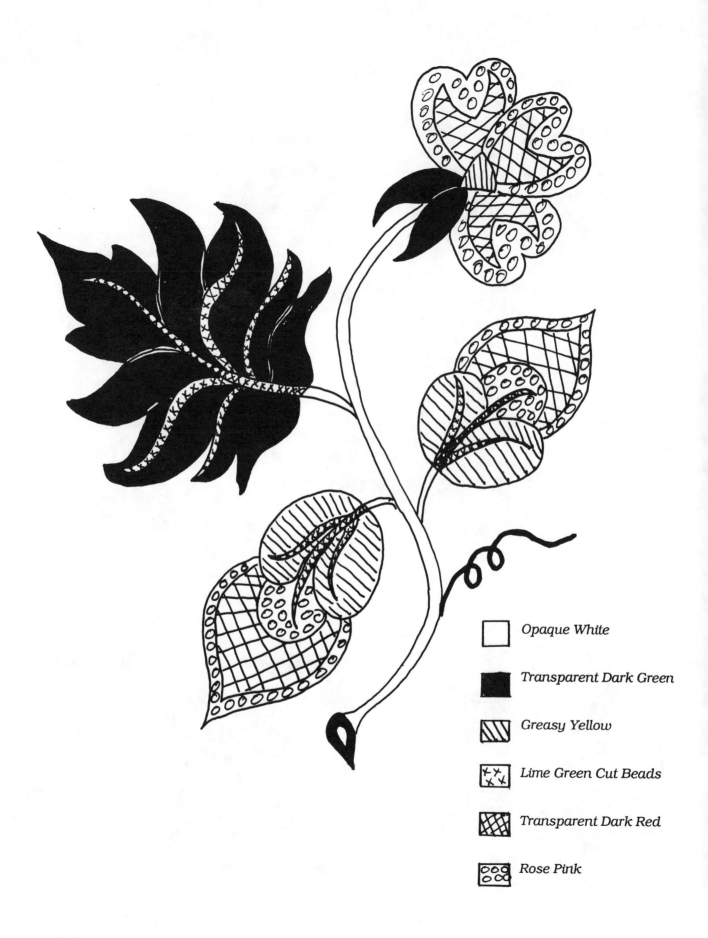

Opaque White

Transparent Dark Green

Greasy Yellow

Lime Green Cut Beads

Transparent Dark Red

Rose Pink

106

THE TECHNIQUES OF NORTH AMERICAN INDIAN BEADWORK
by
Monte Smith

This exciting book contains directions for selecting, buying and using beaded materials; guidelines for either buying or making your own beadwork loom; and, an examination of Indian beadwork designs, their development, significance and uses.

With complete step-by-step instructions for all of the variations of beading techniques used in both loom and applique work, included are directions for beading round objects, rosettes and necklaces.

There are approximately 200 illustrations, examples and photos of beaded articles from 1835 to the present. Examples are from the Apache, Arapaho, Assiniboine, Bannock, Blackfoot, Cheyenne, Chippewa-Cree, Comanche, Cree, Crow, Flathead, Gros Ventre, Huron, Kiowa, Mohawk, Navajo, Ojibwa, Omaha, Otto, Piaute, Pottawatomi, Sac & Fox, Shoshone, Sioux, Umitilla, Ute, Winnebago and Yakima.

This is a book of 102 pages that anyone interested in Indian Beadwork will want to own and study.

NEW ADVENTURES IN BEADING EARRINGS
by
Laura Reid

This fantastic new book is fully illustrated and presents step-by-step instructions on making truly beautiful and distinctive earrings.

Written by noted craftsperson and author Laura Reid, each step is fully explained and the entire text has been "reader tested" and enthusiastically endorsed.

The styles include five-star, snowflake and cross point-style earrings; small fan, large bugle fan, large and small bugle fan, porcupine quill fan and circle fan-style earrings; and, three-square, bugle star in circle, large bugle rectangle, small bugle base, five bugle base, seven bugle base, ten bugle base and one dimensional cube square-type earrings.

All of the materials used are easily obtainable and all of the styles are based on seed beads and bugle beads. Further, from the styles explained and illustrated, and based on the easy-to-follow instructions, the reader is encouraged to go beyond the basics of the book and create their own designs.

Anyone who enjoys creating and then wearing beautiful craftwork will find this book to be a must.